The Origin Comes Alive

At Home with the Divine Presence

Cale Rainer

The Origin Comes Alive: At Home with the Divine Presence
by Cale Rainer

Copyright © 2016-2022 Maleah Publishing

This book is copyrighted with all rights reserved by the Author and Publisher. No part of this book may be reproduced in any form and may not be stored in a retrieval system or transmitted by any means electronic, mechanical, or other, without written permission of the copyright holder(s), except to quote brief passages for review.

Publisher: Maleah Publishing

Editions:
First 2018: Rev 1. 2019, Rev 2. 2019, Rev 3. 2020, Rev 4. 2022

ISBN:
978-0-9996365-0-3 (Paperback)
978-0-9996365-1-0 (eBook)

Published in the United States of America

More about this book: www.TheOriginComesAlive.com

For those who remember

Contents

Introduction.	vii
1 A Sense of Creation	1
2 Remembering the Experience	7
3 Technical Sense	21
4 Losing it	71
5 Religion and the Origin	93
6 Talking to Kids	127
7 Rationalizing it	145
8 Live-Meditation	173
9 Into the Future	187
10 Purpose	201
Glossary	210
Research Sources	213
Contents Detail	214

Introduction

Believers and Atheists alike, get ready to "walk the line" when the Patriarch of life unmasks, showing off his true nature. This observation of direct contact with our origin as it rises in social consciousness created a compelling sense that spawned a worldwide movement known as Religion.

The sense of life is taken to the limits of extreme perspective in this somewhat involved, yet intimate look into our social origin, as childhood memories, open a door revealing the Divine Presence.

This is an introduction to the existence of a Deity that fits the description of what religious organizations call God. A collection of factual and exploratory notes serves as a testament to sharing our sense of origin through the perception of reality; a personal experience telling how we connect with a spiritual entity in our younger years, proving that the reality of God replaces any belief in God.

There are many brief explanations such as: how humans connect with a Deity and why they lose the memory of it; observations of religious ritual methods of worship; how parents should convey the message of this Divine presence of a Deity to their children; and questions arise about the future of a society that might live within the aura of a Divine presence.

Hidden meanings of myth and mysticism are replaced by presenting the truth about life in a straightforward, matter-of-fact way that comes across as very real, and is something that can be believed as inherent in each one of us. No prophetic statements or unbelievable stories of miracles are present, just straight talk and simple explanations about where we come from and how to recapture the memory.

Although the content may appear focused more toward children than adults, it is by no means a children's book. The primary purpose is for everyone, whatever their age or perspective on life, to remember this first sense of life as their origin.

The main subject is intended to be somewhat non-religious, exploring the human social origin through a collection of notes covering nuances of human development that relate to a person's original sense of a Deity-like self. These notes will describe the order of events that shape human behavior from our origin out into the creation of reality. Even though this book contains references to religion, it is more of an educational reference than a message of spiritual guidance.

The goal is to help us understand who we are and where we come from, as well as to help parents educate their children about this phenomenon. Keeping this in mind, it might be helpful to envision yourself as a four-year-old while reading. This version of the book contains numerous technical notes that might be confusing to parents and their children, so you may have to pay more attention while reading these areas.

Rather than a novel with a storyline, it is a unique collection of descriptive notes written as separate instances, and where each instance is directly connected through the Deity but may not always be connected in any specific order. They were compiled and edited over a great number of years and discuss the same subject from slightly different perspectives. Therefore, some may seem repetitive by nature. For this reason, it might be best understood by taking each note individually.

You are about to experience something that is considered uncharted territory and may require a special understanding regarding the accuracy of its content. However, due to overwhelming evidence and through the many perspectives of this Divine presence, the predominant subject is determined to be true.

It is not a psychology or science paper, but a general observation project that stands on its own, unaffiliated with any religion, cult, or scientific group.

This book will describe true-life situations by Locean Simeo and his sister, Melina as they experienced an extraordinary and elusive phenomenon of a Divine Presence in their younger years. It tells of specific happenings based on their notes taken over a lifetime. The Forthcoming chapters are accounts of these notes that not only tell the story of their experiences with a Divine Deity but further explain this phenomenon to be compared with religious accounts from earlier and future prophets and mystics, as well as coupled with specific modern-day scientific facts as they might apply to this subject.

After pondering the many nuances of notes, some of you might think Locean was some sort of prophet or Messiah, yet others might see him as nothing more than a dumb kid with a rather "vivid imagination." In any case, his experiences do present authentic, non-fiction events that, if you can remember, you'd have little trouble accepting as outrageously real, yet believably true.

Read these notes as if they are narrated by Locean with several responses by Melina, from their birth and childhood growing experiences up to the present day. Follow as closely as you can while they take you on a journey inside the Divine Presence to remember some things long forgotten. This is an extremely difficult memory, so most of you will not be able to remember but some might.

It's all in how we communicate that makes the difference in how this subject impacts us! The power of suggestion is the greatest tool on earth and used here to its best end by introducing this forgotten step of our natural social origin.

1
A Sense of Creation

This chapter is a theoretical journey telling how we were brought into this world learning how to behave from an authority greater than that of our parents.

Deity: thing of origin; the Divine; a supreme-being that is all-knowing and seeing; a single character identification supporting multiple behaviors; creator; controller of thought; official moderating the thoughts of its creations; see *father*.

Sometimes it seems as though a step in the development of human beings has been left out, possibly jeopardizing the future of our entire social order. Over the past millennia we have continuously worked toward an evolution from social aggression to peaceful harmony, yet this quest has proven to be an almost impossible task. Nevertheless, we keep trying!

We, humans, have spent a considerable amount of time learning things that sometimes confuse our true purpose of existence. To further understand this, we can observe that some scientists and theologians think that all things may be related to each other. This of course makes perfect sense, providing all things socially evolved from the same point of origin. Keeping this in mind, we could look at ourselves as an example of this phenomenon. Let's look back to the very beginning—before life itself—and explore how we might have become human beings...

Imagine, at one time, there was nothing anywhere except several of my thoughts roving around in the dark, where I played with each of them (kind of like thoughts inside the head). But the thoughts inside entertain me only temporarily, until I feel a void; a space where there is no thought activity; a very lonely space of darkness.

So now I'll need to create some way to make these thoughts lighter and therefore more attractive for play. I will arrange these thoughts in some order of prominence to create one composite thought. This composite thought can now work independently to create and alter the character of all my thoughts to make them interact together. This composite thought will be called a *Deity* and carries a distinct masculine identification of a *Father*.

Next, I'll create a second set of thoughts that are complete opposite thoughts, separated from, yet complementing the first set—which results in a feminine identity like a *Mother*. Now I am a *Deity* with two separate sets of thoughts instead of one. These two thought-identities work cooperatively together to satisfy my sense of loneliness, setting the stage for a space where I can realize a sense of myself opposing myself.

These two opposing thoughts will expand in different combinations and reincarnate into other kinds of thoughts that are further arranged to interact and play with each other in sort of a *go-round* motion, where one of the thoughts remains stationary while the others swing around it. Once these thoughts are set in motion, they create a sensation of excitement or physical feeling realized as a result of this motion. This sensation of motion further results in the expansion of an element of *light*. This action of motion merged with the enlightened element is going to be known as *physical reality* or just *reality*. I will call this new motion of reality, *life*, and define it as the *feeling of being alive*.

I look at this go-round like a tiny family of thoughts where the mother and father are the center or nucleus, and the kids are the elements revolving around it. I am now going to call this family the *atom family*. But after some time, the atom family gets bored and its sensation begins to slow down, causing the light to fade. So, it thinks that it should have some company. It decides to replicate itself and make more families similar to it until there is a whole neighborhood of different kinds of atoms.

These atoms further expand and grow into what we know as microorganisms, and even further grow into creating the earth, air, water, and more advanced life-forms such as animals, all the way up to the most advanced animal: *human*. All of the elements I have just mentioned can now communicate in opposition to one another to bring about a beautiful, light-fulfilling, and satisfying sense of life that can very simply be defined as the *love of being here in reality*.

I can sense myself communicating with other things surrounding me as objects opposing me in reality. I've discovered that these objects of reality can communicate back; sending me signals I can process and then send back to them as if we are exchanging thoughts. This is the creation of a *cycle of thought* that is now firmly established as the interaction of all living things.

I have now evolved into a human being. And soon after birth, as Locean Simeo, my first thought is to interact with objects of my new reality. By communicating the sense of my love of reality, I am teaching myself how to identify with soft, round things; hard, solid things; things that fall to the ground; things that float in the air; things that are wet and those that are dry. Thus far, I really don't know anything about these things; I just know myself. But I do learn one more thing: I discover that my original identity is attached to the physical sense-of-being. This is the same identity I knew when I was a Deity, way back when I was just a lonely thought in a dark space. But now, in the light of reality, I can see a vision of this identity in things.

I perceive this vision through the 'cycle of thought' when I broadcast my memory of this fatherlike identity out to objects of my immediate reality, and as this echoes back, I naturally interpret the objects as a Deity.

2

Remembering the Experience

Remembering: A Sense of Origin

Sometime after birth, a very special experience takes place when a sense of communication with objects of reality echoes the identity of a Divine Deity. This is when you hear little kids going around calling things *dada* or *daddy* as they witness a fatherlike identity appear like a Deity ghost in objects of this reality.

As children, what we called *dada* was an identity-sense and not a graphic image like the face of a man because there is no human physical form connected to this Deity. It is also totally silent, not uttering a word. It does not change character but remains identically the same each time it appears.

This is an identity that is similar to that of a human father but with a distinctly different personality. It is a natural phenomenon primarily seen, on occasion, during early childhood but may continue to reappear for many years thereafter in certain children. It appears as a natural function of the very first thought of life. Millions of people see this every day—it just so happens that the large majority of them are under five years of age.

I can remember enjoying a very special intimacy with a fatherlike reality, where I saw this identity in many things like trees and the sandbox. Melina said she saw it coming from a chair, toys, and a fence. It was seen most prominently with inanimate objects—still-life thoughts were easier to meditate on and more important while experiencing the fatherlike thought of this ghostly Deity. But animated objects such as people and animals seemed to remove this identity through an active progression of thoughts.

The presence of this Father-deity brings with it a joyful, very wide-awake, and orderly intellectual sense of understanding physical reality. But it has something else, too: a strong, sensual feeling of being here commonly known as *grace.* If you could merge all these ideas, you would come up with an overall sense of reality that will be referred to throughout this book as *the Father, the Divine, or the Deity...* This is our sense of origin!

Usually, children, like adults, don't talk about things they don't know anything about. Listen to *goo-goo, aa-aa,* and other strange sounds that come from babies. If you were to ask babies what all these noises mean, and they could talk, they might tell you, *daddy*! Even though babies are trying to mimic other people talking, every sound they make might very well represent the Father, because it is just about the only thing they know. When you hear a baby say *dada* or *daddy*, he or she would say *father* but hasn't learned the word yet.

Gender

In the presence of the Father, gender is not specific, meaning that girls have this experience as well as boys, and probably at equal magnitude. Through observation, little girls should have the same perception of it as boys.

Boys grow up in society learning to be boys, and girls to be girls, and also learn the differences between themselves. And although they are brother and sister, however, they share the same basic identification in the Father's presence. This is what I call a *common human identity*. Except for their physical characteristics, the Father makes them more equal to each other.

A Sense of Manner

When I think of the phrase *love of life*, it seems to represent the greatest thing I can ever imagine. And, as a child, the greatest thing that ever happened was the presence of the Father.

Under the influence of his presence, things that kids see have a masculine persona. Kids don't just look at things and say *daddy*, they grab things, too. This is all a part of feeling the total experience of this Deity, and particularly supports an intelligent physical perception of a gentle flow and loving sense of reality that one could call *graceful*.

When two people sense their joy of reality together, in unison, they have established a very special common bonding that we call *camaraderie*. Everybody has this same original sense of togetherness in common—it's part of the manner of *grace*.

This sense of grace may be the most prominent understanding of the Father that is present in both children and even some adults. If you are familiar with the phrase – *cool, calm, and collected* – then you already understand something about the Father. If you fuse these three words, they equal *grace*. This is the manner of the Father and how it feels to be in his presence.

This sense of manner is my conscious of the origin of life.

The Love of Life

When children call things *dada* or *daddy*, they are energized with the highest form of love; an ecstasy about life and unconditional love of all things. They are not only feeling this total ecstasy of love about their reality but also learning to share this love with others. This is the first step in a child's understanding of social behavior. It appears that the Father is where love originates.

Eventually, we learn not to unconditionally love all things, as we did when we were children, but progressively learn that this love is restricted to those with whom we are most familiar. Later in life, we learn to narrow this to choosing only one person to prominently love as a mate.

Sensing

For those who can remember back this far, you would see that the presence of the Father brings a happy, bright, fearless, and comforting reality where you feel a greater sense of self outside of your physical body. It's a confident, free, peaceful feeling; a perfect state of well-being; a reality that is not childish but more of a combination of adult and child. The extraordinary sense of natural order, coupled with the absolute enjoyment of being here, yields a more adult-like experience rather than one that is childish. This is a mature experience when a person's state of mind reveals that the *unconditional love of all things is better than the love of any one thing.*

The intellect of life in the presence of the Father is by feeling, not just knowing. Much of my knowledge was acquired through physical sensation and not just an act of knowing something from thinking only. While learning to form thoughts at play, school, and work, my thoughts organized things because of the way I felt or experienced them outside of my physical body. If there were no physical feeling, I might otherwise be just like a robot—thinking only and not feeling anything. Thinking thoughts without feeling any physical sensation became greater after learning more complicated thought processes.

Outside Sense

Let's imagine that in the beginning, we had no identity. If we were left with no identity, we might have no sense of life. So, something had to give us a sense of being alive. That alive identity is the Father.

Through my memory, the Father appeared to be separate from the physical function of the self. As a child, he was recognized as a small part of life held inside, but outside was seen very prominently in objects of reality, appearing as a Deity. And because the fixation on his presence outside was so great, he wasn't recognized as much inside.

It's as though, while in his presence, there is only a set of outside feelings, where the Father is understood as an *object of sense* as opposed to that of the self. This is how I perceived his presence in things seen and felt as a baby and for years thereafter.

A Sensual Order

Each child came with a set of commands separate from those taught, progressively by parents and society, since the day of birth. These commands represent specific behaviors that suggest a primary sense of natural order. They are sort of like a predefined set of inherent rules, maintaining social behavior as well as all the necessary functions of the body. These are the commands from the Father that seem to precede everything taught while not in his presence.

The Father has this natural sense of order built into him, and you can feel this order rather than think it. In his presence, there is a freedom of order that differs from that of society, where the order is segregated and regimented by a foreign force of human authority. This sense of a free, self-contained order has established the foundation for camaraderie with one another that we learned while in his presence.

This is kind of like a moral issue by realizing a self-contained sense of order about ourselves and in each other. It's a very confident, loving, and sensual, moral order. When I think about this, it seems strange that ecstasy for the love of all things in the Father's presence would be so directly coupled with such an extraordinary sense of order!

Rite of Passage

As Locean Simeo, a boy enjoying the presence of the Father, I realized that I was at home-base with a familiar, family patriarch providing a secure and loving feeling about reality. But moreover, this very special experience was my *rite of passage* and initiation into life, confirming that I know who I am and where I come from by understanding the commands of the Father, as a Divine Deity, and control my behavior throughout the rest of my life.

Explanations

There are several things I remember about the process of experiencing the presence of the Father over a period of time. The following are explained in order of occurrence:

1. The Original Sense

This is the original sense of life that I knew soon after I was born, where I saw the presence of a fatherlike identity everywhere, in all objects of my new reality. This was my childhood *daddy world*. This father was perfectly silent, had no physical form, was neither dark nor light, and seemed very passive and elusive to the active state of mind of social events.

2. Fading Identity

As I became familiar with things around me, I noticed that my sense of the presence of this Deity would occasionally fade to the point where I could not recognize a father identity at all, yet still felt some residual sense of his presence.

3. Occasional Deity Sessions Return

In my earlier years, the Father's presence would fade but then peek right back at me. Sometimes, he wouldn't come back for hours or even several days. The older I got, the longer the time was for him to return. But when he did come back, he would show himself in short sessions of between several minutes to maybe fifteen minutes or even more.

4. Memory Loss

In between these sessions, his presence was forgotten. If someone had asked me about this, I would not have been able to answer, because somehow the experience of seeing the presence of this Deity was blocked from my memory. However, I now know that it was still in my memory somewhere, but just misplaced. A strange kind of memory loss—I couldn't even remember something right after I did it. Needless to say, this memory is not easily recallable!

After the Father faded from my awareness, I would forget that he had ever existed. Well, at least until he returned, and then recognized him as familiar and happily welcomed his return.

5. Aura of the Divine—Patriarch

After this experience fades away, a lingering, unseen sense-of-being without the specific identity of the Father remains present in one's immediate surroundings.

If any of you can remember, it was like a joyful, brightening *aura of love* about reality in the family and a keen awareness of the presence of something in between us all, like it was communicating through the air, as if to say, *it's where we all came from.* It was more like the head of your family, sort of like your parents, yet it seemed older and in charge of everybody and everything. This sense of a hidden being might resemble the *patriarch of your family.* This was not something that you could see because it was a thought that had not progressed far enough to see any specific identity.

Another way to understand what I mean by the *aura of the Divine* is: even though it is not visible, you'd still sense the identity about the aura of reality and call it *Divine.* But if you could see it, you'd no doubt call it *Father.* This is the thought of reality that some people often refer to as a *third person, the third eye,* or *Jesus.* You'll often hear people say, *Jesus, is really here!* But this is not Jesus. It is the *aura of the Divine* sense of reality.

6. Losing the Aura

We can be aware of this *aura of the Divine* for our entire lives. But sometimes, even it will disappear from the conscious as if it has gone forever. Now we can truly understand the term *losing it*, as it refers to, *never to be seen again.* Nonetheless, unlike the presence of a fatherlike identity, the *aura of the Divine* memory is retained and not lost, meaning it can be recalled when prompted.

<u>Summary</u>

The experience of the presence of the Father was like a ghost that appeared and disappeared at random intervals, from several minutes to one hour, one day, or even months apart as I grew older, until one day it finally disappeared for good, and never reappeared again. This experience wasn't something I asked to happen—I had no control over it. It just happened at random while in a state of meditation and surrender.

There are three different instances of *losing it* that are covered in this book:

1. The visual experience of the presence of the Father disappears.

2. The complete loss of memory of the Father's presence.

3. The loss of awareness of the *aura of the Divine*. (This memory is retained, and not lost.)

There seems to be an almost impenetrable *memory barrier* between the conscious *aura of the Divine* and the forgotten presence of the Father; one memory can be retained, while the other is seemingly gone forever!

Note: These instances are explained from different perspectives within the upcoming chapters, such as: losing it through social conformity; technical explanations; religious and salvation perspectives; and learning experiences for parents and kids. So before continuing make sure you completely understand the foregoing explanations.

3
Technical Sense

Base Memory

Everything we do and create in life comes from the base of what has been recorded in memory. These are *base memories*, such as feeling the grass under your feet, sitting in a chair, crawling, walking, and talking. They soon lead to more advanced forms of action, like climbing trees, playing baseball, and learning math and science in school. Memories are stored in an area of the mind to be recalled and repeated but can also create new ideas from past experiences.

Imprinting to Memory

Children generate an image of this father identity in things they see. This image then makes a permanent impression in the memory that can be recalled later.

Take your thumb and press it on an ink pad and then on a piece of paper. You have just made a print of your finger on the paper. This process is called *imprinting*. In theory, babies and children do the same thing when they call things *dada*. It appears that they are imprinting the original identity of their creation into the memory, and by doing so they are also creating a familiar understanding of identity for everything in physical reality. They won't be able to progressively learn about anything without first giving it an identity. In other words, they see an identical match of their creation in objects of reality in their immediate surroundings—sort of like looking into a mirror.

Mirroring

When you look into a mirror and see your reflection, this will imprint into your memory. This whole process of remembering your reflection is called *mirroring*. This memory becomes an integral part of you and can now work within your thought processes to build an overall persona (vision of the self).

Thoughts are formed through this mirroring process by sensing some of the self in everything seen and learned. And because we were created by both a mother and father, there is a sense of each inside. So, when looking at them, you should see a reflection of yourself in them. This is also true for other members of the family, such as brothers and sisters. However, because we all have a Divine origin too, it would seem that we should also get a *sense of a Divine* mirror from the other family members, as well as anyone else for that matter. But this is not always the case.

The Silent Deity

In the presence of the Father, it is obvious that he is silent. You can see and sense him, but he never says anything. If you were to remark—that he says something—this means that you would get a response via an overall sense, sort of like an intelligent sense interpreted through the creations of reality without any audible sound.

If this Deity was here before human beings, how would he know how to speak to me? This is also true for any visual identity like the face of a man. He can't show his face or speak because he is older than humans, apes, birds, insects, and every other animal on earth. If he were to speak or show his face, which animal would it be—a human, bird, or insect?

I get a strong sense, through this silent communication that the Father is the pure, first thought of life because he was the original thought before life ever began.

Progressive Thought Processing

Human beings have a particular sense about them because they possess the ability to communicate intelligently with objects of reality, in which they can see an intelligent being like a ghost showing itself as a fatherlike identity emanating from those objects.

This is most effective with inanimate objects rather than those that are animated. One reason may be because communication signals can be directed or targeted to a stationary object more easily. But because humans have very special communication abilities, they also can add complex applications stored in the memory to be recalled to interact in current and future situations. This complex thought activity progressively creates situations that act as filters, covering up the original sense-of-being. This will be called *progressive thought processing* (PTP).

This phenomenon of PTP in humans alters the character of communication as it flows through the body, resulting in a change in the overall sense and vision of the human condition, from that of the original sense-of-being of the Father to one that takes on the persona of the person. But inanimate objects, such as trees, bicycles, and furniture, have no or very little PTP to confuse communication with the original sense of a Deity.

ESP

This sensing of the Father may also partially explain a function of frequency communication known as ESP (extrasensory perception). We seem to have the ability to know or control things that happen outside of the individual body, as though they might extend or transmit thoughts to other people and things silently, without doing or saying anything. If you pay close attention, even as an adult, you might be able to sense this.

In the presence of the Father, I can remember communicating with the grass, trees, and other objects. And sometimes it seemed my senses could almost detect things would happen before they actually happened. I felt as though I was sending out signals to things (like radar waves) that would send a reply, echoing my signal. I was keenly aware that there was a very small father identity inside me that appeared as a very large identity outside, which created what I call *the presence of the Father* that I saw in objects of my immediate surroundings (like we were one and the same). But you don't have to be in the presence of the Father to sense ESP. I can remember numerous occasions as a child, and even up into my teens, when this phenomenon of feeling ESP took place while not in his presence.

A True Example of ESP

One day, me and my sister, Melina, who was about the same age, saw the presence of the Father together, at the same time. You would think that each of us would have seen the Father in different places—like Melina would see him in the chair and I would see him in a door—but this was not the case. We both saw him in the same place, simultaneously. This strange coincidence could be because of the *flow of energy* gathering in one place. Energy is communication, and the more communication in a room, in one particular place than another, is why the Father is seen in that one place rather than two different places.

This ESP or telepathy is when one person will pick up on the other's silent communication and suggest where they will see the Father appear as a Deity.

Healing

If you were to scrape your knee on something, you'd know that, in time, it would heal itself. The human body has a built-in ability to self-heal. But sometimes we don't self-heal very well.

Human beings are not perfect, and as a consequence get serious injuries and terminal illnesses doctors can't always repair. They can only administer a high degree of first-aid. Therefore, it's ultimately up to patients to heal themselves.

Psychological problems can be difficult to self-heal. This type of healing is *thought healing*, not physical, so it sometimes helps to use others to aid in generating the healing process. But often, this kind of healing doesn't work very well either, leaving us, again, to heal ourselves.

The more often one connects with the Father; the ability to self-heal should become ever more apparent. Some people even meditate or pray, trying to communicate by opening a *channel* to him in an attempt to aid the healing process. This is like ESP to contact the Father to become rejuvenated with his behavioral elements.

These elements are not just for social behavior, but the behavior of bodily functions, as well. In his presence, it feels like his energy is running through me, relieving me of all my ills. This energy is not just contacting every organ, but every cell in my body. If I get hurt, I will immediately be overcome with a feeling of surrender. This feeling is similar to meditation. This is my attempt to ask the Father to help rejuvenate my bodily organs and to repair me... Such is the process of self-healing through a sense of surrender.

Submission

Submission is a natural function of life that is like giving up processed information acquired from your surroundings. It is the last stage of a process in a *cycle of thought*.

This is sort of like communication when you breathe in you are taking in communication, and when you breathe out you are communicating back out. Everything has an intake and an exhaust, for example, electricity comes from a source and passes through a device, such as a television, that uses the electricity to function, and then the electricity returns to its source. Returning to its source is submission, just like exhaling. Everything in the universe uses this same or similar process of submission.

Submission takes place when you get tired of hanging on to the anxiety of life. Breathing in and holding it creates anxiety. Breathing out relieves the anxiety. Exhaling the air leaves you with a sense of surrender, and a relaxing feeling of inner peace and tranquility.

To feel rejuvenated, you must submit thousands of times per minute—you are essentially submitting information that has already been processed. For instance, when you get hurt or feel bad inside, you naturally will attempt to submit this hurt, almost as if you are submitting a plea for help.

This rejuvenation is like being cured of all your ills and results in a wide-awake, relaxed awareness of life. Each time your thoughts make a complete cycle, you'll be rejuvenated with the Father's energy. If you were to stop this cycle of thought completely, you would experience the final submission: death.

The Vanishing Point

Artists use a method of drawing known as a *perspective* in the process of creating their work. Visualize a row of buildings, where the closest building is large and the farthest away is small. If you were to draw lines along the tops and bottoms of the buildings, they would taper down and eventually converge at one point. This point is known as a *vanishing point*.

All the buildings are drawn by first creating these perspective construction lines from this one point. Any windows, doors, sidewalks, and shrubbery, in turn, are created by the artist from the perspective represented by these tapering lines. The farther away you are from the vanishing point, the more difficult it is to see, until you get so far away you can't see it at all.

All things considered, let's look at the Father as a vanishing point from where all applications and beliefs originated. (It should be understood as the beginning or *source thought* from which all religions have based their commandments and rituals; and from which all thoughts of feeling and intellect were drawn, and acquired knowledge, throughout the years, developed.)

Everything we think and do is added minute by minute and day by day, from this starting point, until we are so full of applications, we sometimes become "full of ourselves" and find that we are also full of problems and have difficulties resolving them as a result.

After Our Design

If aliens from another planet were to come to earth and see, tables and chairs, cars and roads, books and computers, without seeing any humans, they might wonder what kind of specie inhabited this planet. They probably would guess what our physical and mental anatomy was like, by examining the things we make.

Human anatomy has something known as a *brain* that is sort of like a house where people come and go many times throughout the day. But unlike a house of people, the human brain is a *house of thought* that processes and stores information that comes and goes.

So now let's look at some instances that show how human beings process thought similar to the things they make:

<u>Communication signals</u> are broadcast so they can be captured by a radio. The existence of a radio tells us something about the design of humans. Humans are like radios in a certain respect; they put out signals that capture thoughts of their reality, but additionally, process and record them in the brain.

<u>A computer</u> acquires information that is held in a *random-access memory* area (RAM). After this information is processed by this random

memory, it is then moved to a *hard-disk* storage memory area where it can be recalled back into the random memory when prompted. But there is another memory area that neither contains newly acquired information nor stores information: it is called the *read-only memory* (ROM). Unlike the RAM where information can be entered and changed through processing, the ROM information is not so changeable. This ROM holds information that makes up the computer operating system (OS). The RAM would be useless without the ROM because the ROM is the part of the computer that contains fundamental functions that make processing possible.

The human brain seems to work just like a computer: we acquire thoughts from reality that are input to a *conscious memory* area (RAM) for processing. These thoughts are then moved to a storage memory area where they can be recalled when prompted. But there is another area that controls all of the processing of thoughts that come and go from the brain: the *genetic memory* (ROM). The genetic memory is relatively unchangeable and contains the original behaviors of the Father from which all thought processes are based upon.

For these creations to be compatible with human activity, they would have to be capable of supporting the fundamental elements of the Father for each particular application, or else they might be rendered useless!

How did humans ever know how to do all this?... Because this is how humans are made and how they function. Humans have, unknowingly, copied thoughts of their make-up, to reality. This holds true for everything they have created. They literally have created everything, not only after their necessity but after their own basic design, as well.

Father Operating System (FOS)

You might say that the Father, working in harmony with the first, initial basic human thoughts, is like a computer operating system (OS). All future applications of life are developed from this system. As with computers, the OS is useless without the hardware and the hardware without the software; and because the human body is useless without its thoughts, the thoughts are useless without a human body. Just for fun, let's call this OS the Father Operating System (FOS).

Let's say that this FOS is one identifiable thought, like a thought that fathers all other thoughts. It has all the thought elements necessary to generate support for any application created but only within the parameters of the elements it already contains. You could say that it's like a module of thoughts lodged in the brain that generates a live-being sensual experience, which provides self-enhanced motivation to acquire future applications. These applications are added to this FOS as we learn and advance through life. This process is similar to applications that work in cooperation with a computer OS.

How Does It Work?

Here are several theories about how the Father might work intelligently to affect behavior within the structure of the human body, as well as every other life-form here on earth.

1. FOS: The human body contains many different thought functions all working in harmony together. But if it has thoughts already programmed into it at birth, wouldn't you think that the Father—the most prominent identifiable pure thought of reality—would also be made up of many thoughts? In this case, these fatherlike thoughts could be working separately, yet harmoniously, by giving suggestions to all the thought processes. It's more like a composite of thoughts all rolled into one original thought that motivates and officiates newly acquired thoughts. Or you could call it an originator of all thought processes.

2. It's like an integral part of the physical genetic makeup, where the Father is a series of progressive thought patterns used for identification purposes in communication with objects of reality.

3. Electrical impulses flow from outer space through all things here on earth, causing an alive sense-of-being to take place.

These are some very interesting questions, but which one is telling the truth – one, two, three, or all the above?

Fatherlike Identity

By now, you're probably wondering, why the term *fatherlike* identity? First, a difference between things must be established before they can be given any specific identity. This means there must be a plural sense of identity before either can be identified as 'one or the other.' Being *"fatherlike"* then assumes that there is another identity involved other than just a masculine *father*.

The following will now point out how this is understood and sensed, as well as seen in reality. First, let's look inside and see what's in there...

As I recall the presence of the Father, his identity is made up of four behavioral elements: *Authority > Intellect > Order >* and *Love*. This is the order of prominence of the original elements that our dad (human parent) uses to establish and control the "manner" of his behavior. (This begins with a subtle original manner—sort of like *grace*—but can be altered by changing situations.)

The *Authority* delegates its *intelligence* to set *order* to thoughts. The last element, *love* is used to communicate the others into a sense of being alive, here in reality. In other words, *love* is the mode or method of communication the Father uses to create a sense of aliveness about everything. This is seen more like an explosion of thought that assists in broadcasting the other three elements into reality.

Melina replied: "I'll confirm this to be an accurate observation of the Divine Presence. Nevertheless, being his sister and a female, I know that humans are of two separate beings: one *male* and the other *female*. As Locean wrote down the order as *masculine*, I was looking from the opposite side of the table and viewed it upside down. It then became obvious that this was the order of the *feminine* behavior. So now the next thing to consider is that the female is commonly known to complement, and therefore, enhance the male experience in an opposite way, and vice-versa. This means that the female appears to process thought opposite from that of the male. So, for this to happen, the female elements must be arranged in reverse order, now making each complementary to the other. This is the order of prominence of how a female instinctively uses her original behavioral elements: *Love > Order > Intellect > Authority*."

So, now that Melina has brought this to my attention, let's put the two side by side. This is the process order showing how each gender might use them as the *original manner* of life:

MALE	FEMALE
Authority	<> Love
Intellect	<> Order
Order	<> Intellect
Love	<> Authority

Isn't this the way it really is? The male carries a more prominent authority character, whereas the female is more prominent with her love. The male must go through his sense of authority, intellect, and order to use his sense of love. The female does the opposite. The male intelligence might seem more automatic than the female, but this doesn't mean that the female is any less intelligent, she just goes about it in a different way. (There are times when this is a great advantage.)

How often have you heard married couples say that they can't understand where the other is coming from: *How in the heck does she think? — What in the world is he thinking of?* It is obvious that these two different human beings are processing thought from opposite directions.

Let's look at this from a perspective of complements for both a man and a woman: what good is *intelligence* if you can't put *order* to it, and vice-versa? As a man, ask yourself, what does *authority* need the most?... *Love*—because it is the element that is most lacking or farthest away from his sense of authority. So, men are attracted to women who show their love. Women, ask yourselves, what does your *love* for life need most?... *Authority*—This is because women want to be loved by authority, which makes their love feel secure.

This whole scenario shows a genuine complementary attraction to each of the respective behavioral elements of the original fatherlike identity. These complementary elements create a natural activity between them that you could call *polarity*, which is the real reason behind the alignment of these basic behaviors of our origin.

As we develop from babies and the conscious of the presence of the Father, interaction in different social situations will dictate that more value will be placed on certain elements than others. As an example: assuming a total value of 100 for all four elements, if given a value of 90 to *authority*, only a value of 10 will remain for the others; if given a value of 50 to *order*, the others will be left with only 50. As the value of these elements change, they in effect, create different personalities.

When men and women interact in this environment, by constantly changing the value of their behavioral elements, this creates a situation that can very quickly confuse or erase the complementary attraction between them.

Every time the value of elements changes from their original values, perception of reality is modified, possibly causing the loss of one's sense of origin. But by keeping the values in their original alignment will yield a sense of the original manner of life and the presence of the Father—fathering all-natural creations of life.

Polarity

Polarization is when two opposite forces or entities work together to produce an activity between them. These forces have the same effect as two poles of a magnet: when each comes in contact with the other, they create either an attraction or repel each other (this is a technical explanation). But there are other kinds of forces... Opposing relationships of any kind can create a similar sense of polarity. For example, when a cloud passes over a body of water like the ocean, the water becomes more active. But when the sun is out and there is no wind, the water will be calm.

Plant and animal behavior works in this same way. When something happens, a response polarizes the initial action. The position of our moon relative to earth can affect waves on the ocean. If you have trouble believing this can affect animal behavior as well, then why do dogs howl and teenagers run wild on the night of a full moon?

All things, whether alive or not, are subject to the forces of polarity. This same sense of polarity is what identifies the character of all things, from atoms to plants and animals. It also determines the identities of male and female and parent to child.

Short-circuit Behavior

These four complementary behaviors are not necessarily working in unison but in harmony with one another. If they were in unison, they might cancel out each other.

Let's look at an electrical generator as an example: It has two basic parts, one stationary (Stator) and one that rotates (Rotor). As the Rotor rotates inside the Stator, an attraction between the two (polarity) creates an activity known as electricity. The Stator and Rotor never touch each other but remain separated. If the two were to come together and touch, this would cancel out the polarity and burn-out the unit. (In electrical terms this is called a *short-circuit*.)

Likewise, if the behaviors of each male and female sides of the Father were to get too close together, like to represent equal values (as in unison), they would have a similar effect as the electrical short-circuit... As in the case of a married couple, if both target their sense of *Authority* at each other in unison, this might very well lead to a condition lawyers call, *Divorce*: This couple has lost their ability to maintain a complementary attraction of the original alignment of behaviors.

GM: Genetic Memory

Each one of us was born with a substance that resides in every cell in the body known as *DNA*. It holds information inherited from family ancestors. DNA is also known as *Genetic Material.* There are two linear sides to this material, each representing mom and dad's ancestral heredity traits. Additionally, there is a structure holding the DNA together that processes its heredity information: this is called a *chromosome*, which identifies a person's sex as either male or female. Let's call this whole design the **G**enetic **M**emory (**GM**).

As a figurative idea, imagine the mom and dad sides are parallel lines that are connected by the Father at the top. (This should look like a tuning fork.)

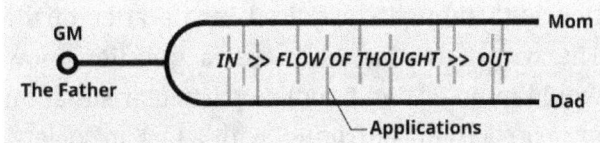

The Father acts as the General Manager of the GM providing a sense of energy, helping to make *applications* from the mom or dad sides. You also might refer to the Father, in this case, as the *patriarch of the family* or the *center of the self*.

As thoughts come in from the surrounding environment, they are processed in response to each current situation. These are the *acquired-thoughts*: the ones learned after birth that are not hereditary. Imagine these thoughts flowing through the Father, then between the two ancestral sides on their way out to be used as response actions.

These genetic traits aid in creating new applications of life that will be used as *acquired-thoughts*. I'm born with many basic instincts that come from both parental sides, and sometimes have no choice trying to change these basic hereditary traits because they are not changeable—I will have to deal with these for life, whether they be good or bad.

But how do I deal with these traits in conjunction with thoughts acquired in life after birth? The way I do this, is to ask a question: how would mom or dad handle a particular situation or task? When confronted with a task in society, to make sense of it, I will go inside my mind to contact the GM to see how mom or dad might handle it. Each time, I will look for a specific thought on either side that matches the current situation. If a match is found, a thought (application) pops out into the flow of thought. This application is then used as an action to help complete the task.

Each time this happens, a new application is created and added to the conscious-memory area, (which is essentially empty until initial thought-applications are created). As more applications of life are added, they act as filters blocking the flow, thus altering the perception of reality from the pure thought of the Father to those needed in response to the infinite number of tasks in society.

A good example of this is that these applications are like photo filters placed over a camera lens. Let's assume that the light coming into the camera is only one color—we'll start with white. If a blue filter is placed in the path of this white light, the white light will turn blue. If a red filter is added to the blue, the blue will turn purple, and as more filters are added, the colors will change, accordingly. This progression of adding filters to alter the original character of the white light is the same process used to alter my sense of reality.

This whole process of bringing thoughts into the path of the original thought of the Father is what gives a sense of progression and *timeline* to life: The acquired-thoughts are based on the GM of my heredity lines, which is based on the four original behaviors of the Father. This is how I perceive the process of growth of my personality—it grows from the common source of my sense of this Deity-father. This is *progressive thought processing.*

If I were to pull back all the application filters, my acquired social personality would be dramatically altered, leaving an open channel directly to the Father; this is when he can be seen in objects of reality as a Deity.

Creating Identity

A *Chromosome* is a structure of the human genome found in every cell in the body and contains what is known as, *DNA* (Genetic Material). It processes mom and dad's hereditary information residing in the DNA.

During the process of reproduction, sex chromosomes are formed by preferring certain dominant elements from each parents' hereditary lines. This determines whether the sex will be either male or female, resulting in a difference in behavioral character for each sex. The male chromosome has both X and Y type chromosomes, but the female has X and X, where some of the male (Y) elements are rejected. In the male, there are both the X and the Y, which suggests it has both male and female characteristics. This is why it's called *fatherlike* and not just *father*... So why do kids call it *dada* (father)?

This may be because of the number of active elements present in the Y (father id.). There are three lesser social behavioral elements controlled by the dominant behavior of *authority*. The X (female id.) has one prominent behavior: *love*, making the other three behaviors more passive as opposed to the very active and dominant *authority* of the male. The number of elements seen in reality that are dominant seems to suggest more of a masculine character than feminine. Although the *love* element is very strong, the other three have enough dominance to call the overall experience, *father*. This is what it looks like while in the presence of the Father.

As a male, and from memory recall, these fatherlike social behavioral elements (which represent the XY) seem to stick out like a sore thumb. The one remaining question is, how does a little girl interpret the order of prominence of these elements? Does she see the *love* element as more prominent than the *authority* and still view the experience as the presence of a father rather than a mother? Melina replied: "It is both, but since the masculine authority appeared to be more prominent than the feminine, I also called it *dada.*"

Gender Identity

I was born with a male physical anatomy, but as I recall, my conscious for life as a baby was lacking any identity as either masculine or feminine. In other words, you could say I was a *gender-neutral* baby. While still in my crib, my parents taught me my very first worldly words: *He* and *She*. And as I grew, I learned how to use the appropriate gender that matched my anatomy.

I started out with a sense of masculine and feminine identification imprinted in my DNA. As a human male, I am known as heterosexual, yet hold conscious thoughts of both male and female, kind of like a dual sex creature (I call myself a *HeShe*, and Melina being a female, a *SheHe*). What I'm saying is that *HeShe* is what *I am*, and heterosexual is how I *behave*.

I did not choose my gender. But through a continuous process of social conformity, I allowed my parents, family, and community to train me how to identify as a masculine person by looking outside myself at my surrounding reality and see gender interactions of others and mimic their behavior.

It's sort of like learning Mathematics: I have the ability to calculate numbers but if nobody shows me how to do it, I will never come to understand it. If I were left alone to choose my gender identity for myself, I would have a fifty percent chance of getting it wrong, leaving me with a SID (Sex Identity Disorder). But if I let myself be trained by my parents and community, I should have a one-hundred percent chance of getting it right—unless of course they show otherwise!

Everything I have done in life has been interpreted through my sense of gender. I can't imagine what life would have been like if I'd been confused about this from the very start. Without proper gender interaction with family and peers, I would not be a properly polarized human-being.

The Projection of Life

Now that the four elements of behavior have been established as to how a male or female might use them, it's time to explore how they might have been used in the creation process for all life...

There is a very special room inside a movie theater called, the projection room. This is the place where a person, known as a projectionist, threads movie film from a reel through a projector so the movie can be seen by the audience on a big silver screen.

Let's look at this by identifying how the four behaviors align with this process of showing a movie: First, the people who created the movie, as well as the projectionist, represent the *authority*. The many thoughts of the movie director, actors, and photographers that put the movie together and recorded it on film, are called the *intelligence*. The movie projector is the *order*. These three behaviors are a male/female contribution yet suggest a more prominent masculine presence.

So now, the projectionist (*authority*) attaches the film reel (that houses the *intelligence*) and threads a length of film through the projector (*order*). It's now time to show the movie... The projectionist flips the switch to turn on the projector; the reel goes around and the film advances through the projector, starting the movie.

But the audience doesn't see anything on the big silver screen! What is going on here?... It seems that the projectionist forgot to flip the switch marked *lamp*. By turning on the lamp, light passes through the translucent film as it advances through the projector, and the movie image appears on the screen.

The light represents the *love* element which appears to be more prominently feminine. If you think about it, the other three elements seem to be very technically active, whereas the light is passive by comparison. The light doesn't seem to own any particular intelligence or order—it's just there. So, you could look at the light as the element that communicates or delivers the intelligence that makes the movie come alive. All the work put into creating and showing the movie by the technical elements is rendered worthless without the light. This appears to be a similar process that creates life- forms here on earth and, quite possibly, everything else throughout the universe, as well.

Common Process

Let's go back to chapter-one and fill in the blanks, where billions of years of evolution were compressed into several paragraphs...

Similarities between the design of the universe and our earth can't be denied. This also tells us that something highly intelligent may be behind this design. If this intelligence is the Father, it clearly shows in these similarities. Let's see if we can break the bond of theory that surrounds this phenomenon and come closer to proving that chapter-one is true—and that a Deity-like supreme-being did create everything in the universe and not just things here on earth...

Activity in the universe, in outer space, is made out of *atoms* that have what are called *protons* and *neutrons* as their centers. Some of these protons and neutrons are electrically charged *(ions)*. The atoms further make up a gaseous-dust cloud, creating a womb-like environment known as a *nebula* that, in turn, makes stars like our sun. The sun, with positive and negative ion charges, radiates these ions out into the universe where a planet, such as earth, can be surrounded by them, charging it with a polarization that creates an atmosphere where life, as we now know it, can be created within that atmosphere.

Next, what we might want to believe is that everything in the universe is only a sense of consciousness with slightly different thought sensations—sort of like thoughts inside the head. They are not considered real until there is a place where they can be transformed. As soon as a place is created, life is "realized." Here within the atmosphere of earth, reality comes alive, by creating things after the same process that took place in the universe.

This process in the universe exists within the atmosphere of the earth in a way similar to a nebula: both are like a mother's womb. Now, you can see that positive and negative charged atoms (ions) in the nebula–womb is a similar process of creation that creates a human being in mom's womb here on earth, by using two elements to create a polarity effect. Except in

The Origin comes Alive 53

mom's womb, they are not ions, they are now a real-life substance known as X and Y chromosomes that are used in the reproduction process. These chromosomes aid in identifying and creating a human being in much the same way as stars are created in a nebula. This means that both the positive/negative charges and the X-Y chromosomes may very well create a fatherlike, or at least a father/motherlike identity as a result of the polarity of their components (X-Y, positive/negative).

The positive and negative charges and chromosomes work together to create a sense of identity here on earth that makes everything come alive. This is when the Father-deity comes alive with a sense of creation.

What I'm implying is that only a conscious thought of the Father may have existed either before or during the creation of atoms and positive/negative electric charges. It's like saying, after this fatherlike identity was created, everything in the universe carried his identity only as a conscious thought, but "realized" to be *alive* in animals and other things only after the earth was created.

The pattern of evolution of matter in the universe, from the very first atom up to advance beings such as humans, appears the same. Everything is made out of the same physical matter and depends upon similar elements to exist. As highly intelligent as the presence of the Father appears to be, it is almost inconceivable that some kind of supreme-being or highly intelligent force isn't behind the creation of all things in the universe. (If this can ever be proven true, then much of what is written in chapter-one is not a theory.) "The proof is in the process!"

The Terrific Twos

One of the most striking observations of the *common process* is the coming together of two basic elements that create or cause some activity to occur as a result of their interaction. This, inevitably, has led to advancing everything in the universe to the next stage of evolution, by following this same pattern.

You might think that computers, we now use in daily life, are highly intelligent. But computer programs are written using only two components: these are, "0" and "1." From only these two digits, an almost infinite number of program variations can be created.

Everything in the universe seems to work using this same design of two elements: protons/neutrons (atoms); positive/negative (electrical charges); XY chromosomes (sex reproduction); 1&0 (computer code); and father/mother (live identities).

Even in Eastern cultures, there is an understanding that all things, both here on earth and throughout the universe, are created and controlled by forces called *Yin & Yang*, which are complementary polarizing situations like, dark and light or even male and female characters.

These two basic forces of life represent a universal code that could be called *the terrific two*s. But it wouldn't be so terrific if one of the elements were missing. This is because each one is dependent upon the other to create and advance any single thought.

The coming together of male and female characters creates a polarizing activity we call *love*: this activity is what creates the sense of being alive! This is a *Universal Love* seen in the presence of the Father.

Male and Female Difference

The only two live-being character identities are, masculine and feminine. To determine the difference between male and female, you can look at both as being HUMAN. If you remove the

HU from the word Human, you are left with MAN, and a natural physical anatomy that matches the masculine sense of identity. And to understand what a WOMAN is, simply look at her natural physical anatomy and you will see a Man with a Womb or Womb Man or Wo-Man that matches the feminine sense of identity.

In Your Dreams

Let's imagine there are two types of dreams: *daydreams* and *sleepy dreams*. Daydreams are conscious, deliberate thoughts from inside the mind that create stories that may or may not become real. Conversely, sleepy dreams happen when you are asleep and are not deliberate, yet sometimes seem very real.

For the sleepy dream to happen, you first have to imagine there are certain parts of the human brain that process thought. There are two types of thoughts: the ones coming in, and those going out. There are also two basic memory areas for these thoughts: *conscious* and *storage.*

Thoughts are processed by the conscious memory area of the brain. Incoming thoughts are temporarily held in this active conscious area during the day, while awake, where they are used for communication, but moved to a permanent storage memory area elsewhere in the brain while asleep. The conscious memory acts sort of like a mixing bowl where thoughts enter from both the storage area and those that come in from activities experienced during the day. Memories held in both the conscious and the storage areas are thoughts acquired in activities after birth (acquired-thoughts).

Now imagine that during sleep, there is a file clerk between the conscious and the storage memory areas. This clerk is responsible for evaluating and sorting the conscious thoughts and then filing each thought in a particular space in the storage memory. During the day the conscious memory is active, meticulously organizing each thought, while the storage memory is relatively inactive. During sleep, this reverses, and most of the activity takes place in the storage memory. While in both memory areas, thoughts are very well organized. The filing process, nevertheless, is a seemingly random process of evaluation, because thoughts would be separately evaluated in order to locate the proper space for each to occupy in the storage memory. If the conscious memory should become slightly active during the evaluation process, you would be aware of these thoughts in the order they were being processed. This results in creating a little movie that we call a *dream*. But because the order of processing seems like a random, collision of thoughts, more often than not, the dream may not make any real sense.

After you have become aware of the filing process as a dream, it will then be recorded as one composite thought, separate from the other individual thoughts and occupying its own space in the storage memory area, where it can be recalled when prompted. This may explain why some dreams can be re-run several times throughout one's lifetime, as they were originally dreamed.

The process of dreaming tells us something about how the brain works in conjunction with the presence of the Father. In your dreams, as new thoughts are being introduced, they automatically make up a sense of an alive situation of motion that appears to be similar to the original creation of life.

Does all life begin with a Father-deity dreaming up thoughts that are just waiting to come alive?

Life is but a dream...
until we learn how to make it real.

Conscious Conflict

The conscious memory area holds temporary acquired-thoughts. Imagine that the membrane walls of this area are made up of DNA (genetic-thoughts). When this area is empty, the DNA naturally floods this area with these genetic-thoughts and with a fatherlike identity as prominent. But when incoming acquired-thoughts enter this area, they mix with the genetic-thoughts. And, if there are too many acquired-thoughts present they will dominate the genetic-thoughts, therein creating an unconscious sense of the genetic-thoughts.

Thoughts of reality come into the brain and are processed for storage. The Father, as seen in objects of reality, is just another thought to be stored, the first time, and all subsequent times you see him appear. But a major problem exists with having to recall this memory. This is perhaps because of a conflict between the incoming acquired-thoughts and genetic-thoughts of the DNA; they both contain this same fatherlike thought and therefore compete for dominance.

After you have seen this Father-deity appear in objects of reality, this will be filed as an acquired-thought in the storage memory area. This, in effect, results in the genetic-thought of the Father being transformed into an acquired-thought.

These Father memories will add up over the years, each time you experience his presence. If you were to try to access the memory of his presence, in a particular instance, then why would you not see him appear in objects of reality instead of just remembering the instance?... This is because you are accessing the acquired-thought in the storage memory area of the brain, and not the genetic-thought which is found in DNA. So, to access the genetic-thought of the Father, you'd have to clear a path to him, so to speak. This is accomplished by pulling back active thoughts in the conscious memory, essentially emptying the conscious memory of all but the most basic thoughts necessary to see the live–presence of reality.

Although this is a very simple analogy, it still may seem a bit complicated. So, here is an example to make it easier to understand: When you look at a tree, this will be a newly acquired-thought held in your conscious memory. Being that the genetic-thought of the Father is already in the conscious memory, the two will merge, and the tree will assume a fatherlike identity;

and instead of just looking like *a tree,* it will look like a *father tree.*

Match-Making

Children see a fatherlike identity in objects of their new reality—even things that appear not to be alive. Because some things that are alive contain male chromosomes, children will assume things that aren't alive will also contain the male identity. This explains how they feel about the presence of the Father, as though everything is really alive with his presence.

When the Father shows himself in objects of reality, this prompts the child to do likewise by looking to the self and says, *okay you showed me yours from reality, now I'll show you mine from within.* When the two meet in the middle, this creates an aura about reality of a fatherlike identity that little kids call *dada.*

But does this father identity truly reside in objects of reality, or is this only a vision in the mind?... Consider, microscopic organisms like insects, trees with leaves, and any new growth of anything alive—do these things come out and say *dada* after they are born? If so, this would suggest that I'd search within myself and match what I see in objects of reality with what is inside my memory. It's like being on the same frequency channel to see the Father appear in reality as a Deity, but those who are not on the same channel will not get this suggestion and won't see him appear. But what exactly is going on inside, to make the match?

Body tissue makes up the walls of the conscious memory area that holds genetic memory and thoughts of the origin, which in effect, flood this area with the dominant character of the Father, who is sort of like the head of the family or *Genetic Manager*. If this memory area becomes empty of acquired-thoughts, it will leave only the thought of the Father. So, in this case, everything that comes in from reality is then interpreted as a fatherlike identity, matching that same identity sensed in objects of reality.

Matching Frequency

This is the ESP that was discussed earlier, as a radio frequency. Are such frequencies broadcasting the identity of the Father from all lifeforms, even those smaller forms of life such as, insects, mites, mold, and microscopic life that can't be seen with the naked eye? These kinds of creatures are born by the millions every minute of the day, right in front of us. As newborns, they haven't learned how to ignore their original manner of behavior through social conformity, and therefore should recognize the presence of the Father, just like our children do.

If you happen to be on the same frequency as these lesser creatures, you will pick up these signals as they pass through walls, furniture, and all kinds of inanimate objects, making these non-life objects appear to emit a fatherlike identity. As the mind takes in these signals, the conscious memory will recognize these and match them with the Father in the genetic memory. This creates an *aura of reality* of a Deity-like being appearing in the objects as a result of a polarization between the objects and the conscious.

The Clay

Let's take different colors of clay and mold them together until we get a rather taupe or gray color. This is how the elemental behaviors of the Father are perceived. It's sometimes difficult to identify any single element because they're all working seamlessly together in harmony. They all work unconsciously, yet simultaneously while in his presence. But in society, we have identified them separately—and figuratively speaking, we have split the character of the Father, so his elements no longer work together in harmony.

I Am Who I Am

Swapping how a person uses the original four behaviors of the Father, in combination with one another, creates different personalities. I might choose to show more *authority* in certain situations or use *intelligence* in others. For instance, if I raise the value of *authority* and *order*, I will take on a personality that may be more like a policeman. But if I use more *intelligence* and *love*, I will show a different kind of personality similar to a doctor. These differing instances happen daily when each behavior element is used, as necessary, to conform to daily activities in my immediate environment.

After a period of time (usually several years) I might become comfortable with one particular combination that seems to support my sense or persona of myself. This is when I realize that I am growing up and permanently altering my overall personality from what it was when I was a child.

I can realize the sense, or vision of my *true self* when I surrender control over my original behaviors—they reset to their original values.

The Origin comes Alive 65

When this happens, my acquired applications pull back from the flow of thought between both genetic heredity sides, leaving only the thought of the Father and the recognition of my original self. This exposes the real person that I am, uncluttered with personalities acquired through social conformity.

This original persona of the self creates a sense of being more grown-up. How often have you heard someone say, *I was more grown-up when I was three years old than I am now.* It's easy to agree with this statement because that's how I felt about life many times, at that age.

The values that changed my perspective on life also changed my vision of who I am. I am the pure thought of me; the human being that I'm supposed to be without any alteration in the values of my original behaviors. There is an original persona that each person should understand about him or herself that can only be truly understood by being in the presence of the Father. In this way, you know exactly who you are and where you come from!

I am who I am, and I am that person who grew from each of mom and dad's heredity sides that gave me my original personal identity before I learned how to change the values of my original four behaviors.

The collective sense of the Father, with all his elements of behavior originally aligned, makes up the joy of life. It's sort of like saying, that if we could raise our consciousness to this level, we'd find that living the whole thing is a better experience than living any one of its parts.

The Spark of Conception

A spark of life that takes place at the exact moment of conception between a father and mother creates a third human being (child) before any heredity traits and social conformity are realized and cultivated by the child. Could this point of conception be what children will occasionally tap into and see in objects of their immediate surroundings as a fatherlike Deity? Could this also be a vision of the *soul*?

Interpreting Existence

Looking at reality from an inside perspective: soon after birth, thoughts of life begin to capture reality and interpret things as a Father-deity. One could only guess that parents did this too, and so on, all the way back through their ancestral heredity lines. This interpretation may also have been passed down through the ages, maybe as far back as one-celled organisms, or anything for that matter, that possesses the ability to reproduce. (Anything that can reproduce is considered to be alive, or at least has a conscious similar to being alive.)

Looking from an outside perspective, this also might be true for atoms that make up inanimate objects like furniture, fences, and rocks where, they too, may very well broadcast a subtle, fatherlike presence out into reality, creating an *aura of the Divine* for animated life to discover.

The interpretation of this Deity, as dada, is the result of the infinite duration of evolution. If all human and animal ancestors did this and believed that everything seen is made from the Father, then maybe this is a sign that all things, including inanimate objects, actually do hold a fatherlike thought. Whether this Deity was the original conscious thought that began the universe billions of years ago, or whether it first began as an alive sense-of-being here on earth, is still in question.

We can only imagine the truth of these statements, but the one real truth that IS NOT a theory or figment of the imagination is the vision of the Father as he appeared in objects of reality in our younger years.

Alive Identity

The Father is the thought that makes the body come alive. If we were allowed to alter this process of feeling alive, our perception of him would diminish. If this perception were to fade too much, one could experience an unlifelike state of being—like a life that's not sensed to be real, where reality seems dark and without joy. It's not *what I am* but *who I am* that distinguishes me as a real human being in physical existence versus a thing of substance with limited or no sense of identity; an identity that is a real-being experience, and one that makes me feel like I am truly alive.

What's the Answer?

Earlier in this chapter, a question was asked: How does it work—is the answer number one, two, three, or all the above? After examining these explanations, it appears obvious that it is, "all the above." But, if you are still apprehensive about these technical explanations, it doesn't matter. What does matter is that the presence of the Father, as a Deity, does exist, and understanding how it impacts our daily lives is something that should not be ignored, at least for the sake of children; the ones who are doing it right in front of us every single day.

4
Losing It

The Father is the simplest thought in existence, perhaps because it was the very first thought. But questions remain for me and Melina... Why did we so totally and completely forget about it? Or more importantly, why hasn't anyone said anything about it?

Everything we know about life, we've been taught: how to eat, speak, tie our shoes, and so on. But no one taught us about the presence of the Father. Young children can't learn about this because it was never appropriately placed in the memory through the normal storage process along with everything else, they've been taught. Therefore, it cannot be used interactively with future acquire knowledge.

It seems obvious at this point that this is the main reason why we didn't remember and never really had the opportunity to use it as our fundamental focus of reality.

Trained

We've been trained to advance into society by looking forward toward the future, but not to look back. What would happen if this Divine Presence from the past were brought into the present?

You took mathematics in school for years, yet after you left school, it seemed that you didn't have much use for it, and therefore forgot much of what you had learned. This is apparently what happened to our association with the Father; we decided this wasn't needed anymore because we only used it to imprint the first step in life. We only imprinted to identify objects of reality during childhood but never associated it with other growing experiences. As we became more involved in the growing and learning process, it became unimportant. So, for that reason, saw no need to further imprint it into the learning process.

Looking back, this left a gap in the basic understanding of life. We advanced many things during the growing process, but often had difficulty associating the manner of our origin along with them.

The Memory Barrier

Looking back at the presence of the Father from society's side, I wonder why any adult would want to live life bonded to him and not advance his or her social conscience? But looking from the Father's side out onto a conformist society, why would anybody ever consider leaving behind the joyful experience associated with his presence in favor of a life in society? Figuratively speaking, you could put a brick wall between these two because they are so unrelated. One is a joyful, super-alive sense of your surroundings, and the other is one heck of a lot of hard work and pain.

There appears to be a *memory barrier* that separates these two different outlooks on life. This barrier exists, in part, because of the original design of the human mind. The mind holds information acquired after birth in random-altering conscious memory areas, while the genetic memory holds ancestral traits as well as a sense of creation. Awareness is focused more on processing thoughts in the conscious memory than thoughts of the genetic memory, making a memory recall of the genetic thought of the Father almost impossible—unless of course, you were to see him in reality at least once, and then imprint that experience to the storage memory.

Perception of Reality

In theory, the conscious thought of the Father is masked through an overlay process of thought applications (PTP), by concentrating on each specific application. More and more applications are added until his identity ultimately vanishes. After much of this takes place, a personal identification develops without any conscious awareness of a Father-deity origin attached to it. This loss of 'consciousness of origin' consequently causes confusion and anxiety, and can even cause severe mental problems.

Children lose the memory of the Father's presence at an early age by becoming preoccupied, and then overtaken, by too much active thought processing. It's sort of like thinking too many thoughts too fast. Adding these applications to the memory too fast alters the conscious state of being, which leads to a progressive change in perception of reality. We can observe that at about the time a child enters preschool, any sense of a Father-deity origin begins to fade more and more into obscurity, and the *graceful reality* of these experiences of his Divine Presence may soon be lost and possibly never seen again.

The Stumbling Block

A primary building block of life should have been established as the first step in understanding who we are. Instead, a contest between social conformity and the sense of origin ultimately created a huge stumbling block, which foiled the perfect development of this first step into society by blocking the thoughts of origin. This whole process turns out to be a rather awkward "rite of passage" for kids, who will soon be growing into adulthood without any memory of the Father's presence and where they come from.

Contest of Conformity

Conformity is, very simply, defined as responding to one's surroundings. As a result of this conforming, we always try to surround ourselves with a flow of life that is favorable to our enjoyment and progress of life-supporting activities.

We chose ideas from society because they were popularized by someone telling us about them. In doing so, we've been led by a conscious effort to concentrate on life applications, and thus, have been brought up in society trained to often think selfishly. This outlook on life has taken precedence over our natural association with others. Consequently, we rudely find out that we have been set up to expect so much of each other that we aren't allowed to touch each other, so to speak.

Everything learned is based upon our association with our first sense of life, yet at the same time dependent on conformity. We, humans, have become products of a standard of conformity that has eliminated the memory of the Father from our understanding of life, and therefore, never get a handle on our true source of identification.

If this memory were popularized early in childhood, kids might be more aware of the Father as a constant reminder of their origin, assisting in guiding them through all newly acquired social activities during a natural process of conformity. Popularizing through training should alter the competitive nature of conformity. This *contest of conformity* may be one reason why we lost the thought of the Father and are unable to remember.

A Sense of Shame

Occasionally, thoughts will disagree with a certain conformist situation, causing a feeling of shame. These kinds of acquired-thoughts are interpreted and compared to be compatible with the genetic memory. But acquired-thoughts are not alive and therefore cannot feel shame. When I feel ashamed by a specific happening, this sense of shame only comes alive when it is activated by the genetic memory and the Father... So, the Father (the alive sense-of-being) ends up taking the blame by feeling shamed.

Shame through Conformity

As Melina and I grew, we imprinted on other people, and in doing so followed the face of their conformity. During our growing years, conformity proved to be the ultimate preemptive power of suggestion. And thus, almost as an accident of development, we were trained away from our sense of origin, which became passive, preferring the more active social conformity instead.

In the beginning, everyone feels good about his or her association with the familiar personality of the Father, because it is obvious that from the start of life this is what generated the original sense of self-esteem. But on the other hand, we often have difficulty with conformist esteem.

The Father became the first shame because, in our early years, we couldn't keep up with the first few acts of social conformity. And once this shame was cultivated, it too became familiar and was copied to acts of social conformity for the duration of life.

The consciousness of the Father-deity was never made part of the social conformity system, and for this reason, a child will learn to feel that he or she isn't allowed to show it. In this way, children are protecting an image for which they don't want to be known. This scenario has been allowed to repeat itself throughout one's lifetime. This is called *Shame through Conformity Syndrome* (SCS).

We have alienated ourselves from our sense of origin, and consequently from each other, by SCS. This has led us into a state of mind where the process of a shamed conversion into society undermined the conscious existence of a very special joy of life experienced while in the Father's presence.

Inside-Out

Both Melina and I agree that we originally knew the Father as most familiar when sensed outside of the body. But as we grew, and learned to think and feel more from inside, any sense of him also went inside. He eventually became more familiar bottled up inside rather than sensed outside around reality. All thoughts that work outside are non-possessive, including the Father. This is probably why he appeared to be more unattached from the sense of self while in his presence.

During our growing years, thoughts were progressively formed by society, where we learned to react to these thoughts as feelings from within. However, there is a consequence to this: through social conformity, one can learn to feel ashamed of sensing the Father outside, therefore, he is held inside to cover up the shame.

So, we are now left with a choice: learn and feel everything we conform to outside and keep a closer relationship with the Father along with everything learned or continue on in society keeping him buried inside.

What we are trying to say is that all conformity might best be cultivated using the conscious of the Father as one integrated ideal, and not for conformity to be allowed to become so totally segregated from the Divine sense of origin by feeling and learning from inside only. As children grow out of infancy and begin to feel intellectually functional, any sense of the Father fades and in many children will disappear completely at a very early age, never to be seen again.

To summarize: Too much thought conforming creates too many reactionary thoughts, which can cause inside feelings to imprison thoughts of the Father, resulting in the loss of what we call the Divine Presence.

Response Thoughts

Shame–based reactive thoughts can make you feel life from within, which restricts the overall Divine experience. Feeling bad is the result of thoughts of the origin being compressed inside. Doing things that decompress these thoughts makes you feel better about life. These origin thoughts seem to come alive when sensed outside of the body in communication with reality, as previously mentioned.

Too much thought progression introduces trying experiences that can cause an overabundance of negative (unfavorable) responses, and consequently, these negative reactive responses lessen the overall physical and mental sense-of-being; or you could say that they render us senseless.

Senseless

We have been taught to know about life but not about sensing life. This has been repressed within each of us by moral-order standards we've learned while growing into society. Furthermore, because our parents didn't know anything about a Father-deity, we never had an opportunity to pursue a natural, sensuous life over the regimented one we were taught.

In the presence of the Father, life is sensed outside. But as we age and lose this sensation, we begin to feel and sense things from within. As we increasingly feel life from within, a keen perception of reality becomes progressively reduced. Maybe this is because the more we learn complex reasoning that produces a sense of knowledge out of a simple life, the more outside physical senses will fade.

Losing by Default

The only real proof of the existence of any thought is that it has an identity. And the primary thought of existence that I acknowledged during my early years, as a specific identity, was fatherlike. So, because this was the most prominent identity known, as a baby, it was only natural that the presence of a Father was seen in everything.

But, as I grew and identified objects of physical life (trees, toys, and so on) and learned their names, I found that playing with these objects became more important than the thought of the Father that was originally imprinted while in his presence. It's almost as if my memory only had so much space, and as more and more objects were added, the Father lost out to them by default, until I finally couldn't remember his presence at all.

It's kind of like adding layers of applications to life that eventually covered up the memory. The last (most current) memory becomes the most important because it is easier to access. Certain thoughts from years ago can be harder to access because they are deeper in the memory, or just never important enough to remember.

No Mirror

When you see something, you will copy it to your memory. And when you look into a mirror and see your reflection, you will copy that to your memory. Thoughts are formed from what is learned through this mirroring process by sensing a bit of the self in everything learned. Each one of us initially learned our relationship to reality through the presence of the Father. But try to get a mirrored sense of origin from a person, especially one who is older!

As we grow up out of infancy, it is difficult to detect a likeness of the origin in others to use throughout our growing experiences because it is overshadowed by heredity traits and social conformity.

This lack of a mirror from others can lead one into being ashamed of not being equal with others in a socially conformist society. It appears we have unconsciously linked our original experiences in the presence of the Father to our association with others in social circles, realizing that we are all actually the same person, learning to expect others to be just like us, but soon rudely learn that they aren't.

Baby ID

I wonder if all kids over the age of about five who hear younger children call things *"daddy"* think it's stupid. This might confirm the point of conformity when kids at a certain age want to move away from anything that represents being like a baby. As they "put down" younger children for this, they are, in essence, refusing to grow up with the Father, so they unconsciously discard his memory. This is all part of the process of conforming away from their sense of origin, which strongly suggests the need to grow up, by conforming to the order of those who are older.

People grow up trying to ditch their baby identification which they directly associated with the Father, and in doing so, also ditch the graceful reality of his presence. The thing that makes me an adult, when I grow up, is my sense of camaraderie and grace (my father identity within). Otherwise, I might remain the baby image that I received by mirroring mommy.

The most prominent memory of the Father's presence was mostly during the baby years. I never conformed backward, but always forward as I grew; and as I conformed forward the baby image was dropped, and consequently, this memory was lost along with it.

De-Fathering via Mothering

Several basic personalities are progressively created from one's original familiarity with the presence of the Father, such as mom, brother, sister, friend, and foe. As we grow up interacting with these, we no longer have a use for any original sense of the Father. And the more we accept bonding with these personalities, the more we unknowingly alter our perception of reality.

There are times that we've created a mother-like rather than a fatherlike sense for growing into society and therefore developed society-conformist standards because of a nurturing in that direction.

We were all born under the influence of a mom-like mirror, experiencing life from her perspective as we grew up through early childhood. Our fathers (human parents) came into life under this same influence and grew from a mom-like mirror too. So, for children to get a true mirror-sense of the Father origin, they must use themselves via their experiences in his presence. You'd think that a human father would be a great mirror, but unfortunately, this hasn't proven to help children understand their link to the Father origin.

The Father, fathers everything we do in life until a mother takes over and presents a continuous learning process. Because knowledge has been mothered into us so much of the time, it has resulted in preempting a conscious fatherly sense of origin. Down through the ages, it is plausible that this has been genetically bred into society.

Do we carry a mom-like nurturing authority type of identification throughout our entire lives in everything from religious faith to school and work? Do we go around mothering thoughts of the Father much of the time?

Society often refers to things as a *mother*: The *Mother Ship* and *Mother-Nature*. Can you see a pattern here? We were brought up from birth believing in a mother mirror image rather than a fatherly identity. If we were brought up remembering the Father and learning our association with him, we might be calling things *father* rather than *mother*. For example, *He's a good ship* or *Father-Nature*. This sounds really weird by comparison. But now that we understand something about the presence of a father identity appearing as a Deity in objects of reality, Father-Nature makes more practical sense than Mother-Nature.

Another observation: as a child realizing total enlightenment, by returning to the Divine Presence of the Father, I had to back up through the mother-nurturing image. And, because *mother*, in this case, acted as a teacher who represented a dominant, feminine physical identity, confusion was created with the fatherly thought-identity of my origin. So, because of this conflict between dominating father and mother identities, complete salvation, and enlightenment (in fatherlike religious terms) would be very difficult for anyone to successfully achieve.

Fear of the Unknown

I had no trouble enjoying the Father's presence during the light of day. But at night, when it got dark, his presence was more difficult to see. When a similar incident was sensed at night, the visual identity became more difficult, and I only sensed the presence of a dominant masculine authority that was missing a feminine love element, which resulted in a feeling of being haunted and terrorized. This fear imprinted into my memory, and from that point on became a hidden consequence of the Father's next appearance.

Moreover, I unwittingly may have inherently and through ESP picked up on this fear from parents and peers who went through this same phenomenon when they were toddlers. Children don't know where they come from. They can become afraid because parents never could nurture the thought of the Father for them to become comfortable identifying at night when they had trouble seeing him... This *fear of the Father* was never taught! It's sort of like a fear of association with something unfamiliar.

Because parents, as well as others, don't provide a father image support identification, young children consequently are caught between the fear of the Father (unknown) and fear of social conformity (also unknown) both at the same time. All of this has contributed to blocking any thought of the Father-deity origin.

After a child has had a traumatic experience of fear associated with the Father, this trauma will be carried deep inside for the rest of his or her life. A modern term for this type of fear is *post-traumatic stress disorder*. Could it be that all of us are suffering from this phenomenon?

The Steps of Knowledge

Very simply, the further away from the Father you get, the further away from the joy of life you will find yourself. You could look at the joy of life as light: the further from the light, the dimmer it becomes. This also applies to social conformity. The more you conform to something, the less aware you are of that to which you are not conforming.

As another example, let's look at climbing a set of stairs: You start on the ground floor, and as you ascend, you're concentrating on each step in succession, being careful not to fall back down. The ground floor is understood as the presence of the Father and the steps represent acquired knowledge of life. With each step, you learn something new. The more you learn about each step, the more your focus of awareness then shifts to the step above. This not only draws your interest in climbing the stairs but also draws your attention away from the Father on the ground floor.

Obsessive concentration for learning (*the process of reason*) preempts the awareness of the Father. So now, the higher up the steps you go, the further away you will be, leaving you with a dim or lesser feeling for life and losing the sense of his Divine Presence.

Rules of Nature

'Suggestion' is the most powerful tool on earth. If we are not careful of what we conform to, the current state of all human civilized order could be jeopardized!

1. Cooperating Masculine and Feminine activity creates the sense of life.

2. Life grows and prospers through Social Conformity.

3. Social Conformity is dependent upon interaction of certain forces.

    a) Voice is the Mother of Social Conformity.

    b) Choice is the Father of Social Conformity.

4. Misuse of the elements in #3 might retard or even cancel #1 and #2.

5. In the balance of Nature the Checksum is always zero.

<u>Melina Summarizes:</u> I think what Locean is trying to say in these rules and several other notes is, that the Divine Presence is a marriage of masculine/feminine thought, forming the foundation for each person's sense of order. And if your sense of origin becomes corrupted by society and your polarizing elements of life swing way out of balance, maintaining a conscious of the Divine Presence may be the best way to reconcile and repair the imbalance.

Orphaned from Our Origin

We have been trained away from any familiarity with the Father by being stripped senseless through the contest of conformity and shame; not recognizing a mirror image of the self in others; fear of unknown feelings and senses; regressing into feeling like a baby and stumbling over the very first step in life by not placing enough value on the Father's presence to even make it worth remembering.

Each of the above situations contributed to holding us back from either returning to experiencing his presence or remembering it ever took place. As it appears, each of us grew up into life's activities through social conformity, by losing both the sense and the memory of the Father, leaving us hopelessly orphaned from our origin.

After listing all the reasons why this memory has been so difficult to retain, the most prominent simply may be that nobody told us to remember! It would be virtually impossible to understand our natural origin without this memory.

5
Religion and the Origin

Although this book is considered somewhat non-religious, there exists a coincidence, because the word *Father* is also used by certain religious organizations. There are numerous diverse religions throughout the world, some of which may not particularly use 'Belief in God' as the foundation of their activities. This book is referring to the ones that do believe in the existence of God as a supreme being or Deity.

Because my sister and I learned from our parents, who were baptized into the Christian Religion, and because this religion seems to explain things more closely matched with the presence of the Father, I will use it as the primary reference in this chapter and throughout the rest of these notes.

The word *God* has been used very loosely. In fact, it is used so much in every aspect of life, you'd think there really is one! So, let's explore this further and discuss some similarities between religion and the presence of the Father that has been around since the beginning of time.

Charade or Real

Some people believe that Jesus and other religious prophets never really existed but are part of a myth, and what they were preaching, *faith through miracles* has proven to be nothing but a charade.

Whether Jesus and other prophets are real, or if they were only characters of myth, is of no concern. It's their message that is important and not circumstances surrounding a prophet or myth that will tell the real truth.

So rather than belief in a myth or the existence of a real person, the best way I can approach this is to look at each instance as a story. These stories can be either a myth or a definitive happening. Religion is telling us stories that act as lessons in behavior; it is about teaching humans how to behave, by using the original elements of their origin. In doing so, they are obsessed with the idea that these elements of behavior originated with a supreme being they call God.

Putting all ritual and belief aside and examining the information that has been collected by religions from all over the world, there appears to be very few, if any, errors in what has been written describing God, regarding the process of realizing him.

Over the past thousand years or so, writings about God have, as crazy as it may seem, weathered language and other changes very well. You'd think changes in language interpretation, as well as different perspectives of belief, would have created a continuing charade. But quite the opposite has happened! Comparing memories of experiences in the presence of the Father with historical documents has proven timely interpretations to be reasonably accurate—at least for the more prominent religions of the world.

The Difference

Over the past millennia, religious orders have performed an admirable task of creating a center of community, charity, and positive, uplifting self-awareness among people as best they could in the face of overwhelming human adversity. The one major difference, however, between *Religion* and *the presence of the Father*, is that religions attempt to explain what it's about in somewhat of a superficial way, while these notes are directly identifying present-time events.

These are two completely different ideas, yet each supports similar components. One is a method of ancient belief through faith and hope, and the other is a straightforward approach through direct memory of current experiences at home. And, since some religions might be giving confusing proof of a Deity from ancient texts, many people who attend church regularly may still be somewhat unsure about the existence of God as a supreme-being or Deity.

Going to church every week is supposed to bestow upon us a sense of our "Father in Heaven." But how often have you left church and not felt any love of the Father, yet at times, quite the opposite? And how many loving, impressionable little kids have found church to be somewhat of a hostile social environment to endure?

The truth of salvation is found within each individual to hold or seek for him or herself. This is the real, true path to realizing the Divine Presence. But would it be better situated in a collective educational environment founded as the salvation for all? Maybe this is what is meant by religions when everyone is involved all at once.

This seems like a good practice because it at least keeps the idea alive.

As we grow older, we can become more aware of the need for a special togetherness with others that brings back the brightening sense of the *aura of the Divine* that was so familiar when we were younger. Many churches throughout the world do give a feeling of love and togetherness even though they might not thoroughly understand the reality of the presence of a Father-deity. It could be that these kinds of organizations provide a place where people can enjoy being together through song, dance, and other things that allow them to communicate with each other in a positive way without any education through belief.

These are the kinds of life-fulfilling actions that lead to a loving meditation of being here *now*, and that if followed by deep personal meditation, ultimately could lead to being conscious of the Father's presence (This would most likely occur in kids). But being entertained through the Father's presence proves a very intimate, personal experience that couldn't easily be mimicked or realized in unison with many people.

Some religious orders see unison as regimented social conformity, not personal. This is the difference: they are only pointing "the way" through acts of unison worship that, at best, result in the awareness of the *aura of the Divine* about reality, but don't go far enough to recognize a child's daily personal experiences in the Father's presence.

Make-Believe

Without the memory of the Father's presence, we are reduced in our perspective of self-awareness, and therefore find ourselves limited to beliefs through faith and hope that are supported by religions all over the world.

It's like believing in something for which we have an intuitive sense, but don't know for sure what it is; sort of like bowing and praying to a shadow of life rather than the real thing, or like playing make-believe.

In our early years, we both went to church many times with our parents and learned what church people were talking about: someone called God, who we came from but couldn't see... One Sunday the parents went to church, leaving Melina and myself at home with a sitter when Melina suddenly saw the Father appear and said to me: *"Why are they going to church to play make-believe for something they don't know ex-*

ists when they could be here with me enjoying the presence of the Father? If this is what religions are talking about, why don't they say so in the first place? Why do they believe through religious ritual, rather than talk directly to each other about their memories of childhood experiences with the Father?" (Re-read the previous note.)

Ancient Ritual Fear

Ancient civilization's worship of pagan objects and iconic Gods possibly demonstrates a fear of a Father-deity they experienced from objects of reality. Many of their reality's elements were worshiped as sacred, such as the moon, sun, clouds, animals, and trees.

It is plausible that some of the very first people to set foot on earth were familiar with the presence of this Deity. But they also may have experienced a very prominent live-being authority associated with this Deity, and then, for some reason, became afraid of it. This could be true if they never were taught to become comfortable with it—perhaps because they hadn't yet developed any intelligent language communication. So as a result, they would have overreacted, dropped to their knees, and began worshiping this live-being authority, both in ignorance and in fear of it.

Just like the "fear of the dark" that I experienced as a child, they certainly must have felt the authority-order of some kind of alive thing in their presence at night, in the dark. The lack of light at night removed the love element from their perception of the *love and order* of the total fatherlike experience that they might have been familiar with during the day, leaving only an *order-of-authority* element, which consequently left them in a state of fear.

One can only imagine that to aid in eliminating this fear, they would experiment by lighting fires, dancing, chanting, and in general, creating exercises in "progressive thought processing" that they found would make this scary, live-being authority go away. They were, in a sense of speaking, "exorcising the demon" in them to drive out their fearful thought of a father-devil authority. And, in doing so, they unknowingly "burned a bridge," destroying their security link to their natural social origin by misinterpreting the Father with all his elements in place as one integrated unit. They also unknowingly set the stage for this to happen for all generations to come!

Over time, through this process of exorcism, and as they gradually lost their sense of the Father's identity by separating his authority from his love, they ultimately formed more advanced forms of ritual–worship, and then became possessed by proxy methods of belief. After this father-identity faded, it left behind only belief, and through attrition of this consequence, faith and hope were born. From this explanation, it's easy to see how pagan ritual–worship is similar to modern religions.

If the foregoing is true, then it seems that by nature of ignorance, we've learned to worship Gods not only because we loved our association with the Father's presence, but moreover, because we feared it!

The Mood of Ritual

For thousands of years, religions have been carrying around beliefs about man's origin that have never been emphatically proved. It is apparent that throughout the history of civilization, many people have been either partially or totally unwilling to comply with the rules of these beliefs.

Is something wrong with this scenario, or is there nothing wrong with it? In either case, there must be something going on, for entire civilizations have been, and still are, possessed by a *rules-of-belief* ritual methodology as an attempt to restore to their conscious, 'the love of the Father in heaven.' This is because the ritual method of worship is just the first step in a conscious effort to induce submission. Another way to say this is that these ritual methods of worship are simply aids used to get you in the mood for submission, and without a certain degree of submission, the connection to our origin is lost.

Looking from an outside perspective, rituals appear to cloak the idea of a true connection to the origin of life, leading many people to believe that this whole idea of worshiping God is a ridiculous hoax or charade. But once you know about the presence of the Father, you'll see why ritual–worship exists, and therefore, understand more about why religion exists.

Belief, Faith, and Hope

Just believing in a higher authority can create a humble, peaceful, and confident sense of life. And life becomes an even better experience when you find yourself surrounded by those who also believe. But some people still have trouble accepting belief, faith, and hope through ritual methodology as a part of the process of worship. So now let's take a time-out and set the record straight about these attributes of life...

When I think of *religion,* the first word I think of is *belief*—the two are synonymous. Faith and hope are dependent upon the system of belief, and belief is a product of *want*. It's about wanting something better than what you have now. Although *belief, faith,* and *hope* are only modifying analyzers rather than something of real substance, they do serve an important purpose: They are used in religion as an attempt to bring forth the thought of God and the calm joyous *aura of the Divine* reality associated with God.

But if you think about it, these modifiers aren't just religious-oriented; they are also used in the process of doing just about anything. They appear to support most phases of life applications. As much as we know, these are used by everyone in times of need to accomplish certain feats, especially the ones that seem impossible.

As an example: during the process of building something, we *believe* that our designs will be adequate and work well; we place *faith* in others that they will be successful in accomplishing their tasks; and we *hope* that, in the end, all will work out okay... If there were no religion, we'd do it just like this, anyway!

Once we know about the presence of the Father, it is easy to understand that God is not a product of religion because there is no belief involved. God was around long before religion, and yes, so were the process modifiers, belief, faith, and hope.

Now the only thing left to consider is that "impossible feat" of *loving* life. To do this, all belief, faith, and hope must be surrendered and replaced by a conscious for *loving now*. At some point, you must stop *analyzing* and start *doing*. *"You won't always get what you believe in, but you will always get what you do."*

Prayer

If you are an Atheist, reading these notes, you might wonder how anyone would allow some preacher to pray over them knowing that God (the Father) is doing this all the time. Why should they let someone else take the place of God?

This is a very good question, and the answer is simple. The basic idea is found in the word *humility*. If you can humble yourself in the presence of another person, then you should be more than able to humble yourself before the Father—at least this is the strategy. A preacher is then acting as a proxy–Father, in this respect, working to administer the grace and glory of God to those who might have difficulty doing this for themselves.

Nevertheless, many people don't like this idea of others praying over them, because they are either atheists and don't believe in God or just prefer to contact their God directly or by some other means. Regardless of whether someone prays in your place or not, you are ultimately the one who will have to let the meditation and surrender process happen if you want to gain results from prayer.

Prayers are like wishing for something that offers the very best sense of life. If you think about it, praying is merely an act of submission in an attempt to contact some kind of Deity-like God; and further, the act of praying is somewhat of a gamble, because it doesn't always work. But it's the trying that gets you in the mood to accept better things to come.

If you like prayer, try this: bow your head, close your eyes, and try to remember your experiences in the presence of the Father when you were a child. This may be the very best prayer you'll ever learn!

Or, if you're deep into meditation, try meditating on your memory of the Father's presence. It might be possible to meditate your way right back into it, where you'll see his presence again. If you can do this, you won't be alone. Other people experience the presence of the Father every day, right before our very eyes. However, it should go without saying that the large majority of them are under five years of age.

The ultimate viewpoint on prayer is that it is best suited to a total sensual environment, where that environment, within itself, is the prayer. This is what reality is like, right before, and while in the presence of the Father. The experience of his presence is like living the ultimate prayer!

The Church

There are times when we refer to *The Church* as the organization of a particular belief such as Catholic or Baptist. But most people think of the Church as a place where they go to worship their God. To clarify this, the Church is a place; the physical environment of one's immediate surroundings; objects of reality. This place can be inside a building with walls, floors, and ceilings, or even outside in the back yard surrounded by trees, flowers, grass, cars, bicycles, etc.

Now, what does the Church have to do with the worship of God?... In times of deep, loving meditation, the Father (GOD) will show himself in the Church. This is also called *The House of the Father*.

The Holy Ghost

If you are familiar with the Jewish and Christian religions, this should be pretty simple to figure out...

The Jewish religion, known as Judaism, was around long before Jesus was born. It has brought forward some interesting notes, one of which defined the social origin of man as a father image, and that this father created all things in his image.

The Father not only appears like a *ghost*, in reality, he shows you a few things too: he appears to be greater than life itself; his presence gives you the understanding that he created you as well as everything you see; he is also highly intelligent like he knows everything about you and every move you make. A great word to describe him is also a religious term: "Almighty."

This *ghost* is what you would call a Deity, as described by religions, but more often referred to as God. (The word 'Deity' actually means 'thing of origin' or 'presence of the origin.') These descriptions are maintained by religions and held sacred and worshiped through meditation. Maintaining these observations of the Father's presence is known as, being *holy*. Now, there is enough evidence to go ahead and call the presence of the Father as he appears in reality, *"The Holy Ghost."*

Let's put together another term: *The Father* is the identity of a Deity as seen in objects of reality, sort of like a *ghost*; my relationship to this ghostly father is like a *son*. If you are educated in the Christian religion, you've probably already guessed this one: *"The Father, The Son, and the Holy Ghost."*

Children of God

Even before Jesus was born there was a rumor going around that a savior was coming to save the world from death and destruction, so to speak. It is accepted that the term *Son of God* existed in religion before the coming of Jesus, as well as talk of a savior. According to the Bible,

Jesus was more than just a savior, he proclaimed himself to be the Son of God.

The rationale for the Son of God is really easy. If you are born a male, your relationship to the Father—as seen in objects of reality as a Deity—is that of a son. So, Jesus realized himself to be the Son of God when in the presence of the Father. Any boy who realizes this same experience would also be called a Son of God; and a girl, a Daughter of God. Because every one of us experienced the Father's presence at one time or another means that we were sort of like Jesus: The Sons and Daughters of God. This is why all people are referred to as, *The Children of God.*

God Loves You

You'll oftentimes hear people of religion say, *"God loves you."* How do they know God loves them when they don't even know there is a God, but only believe there is one?

Previously, in these notes, the love of the Father was introduced as appearing in objects of reality. But an object of reality *loving you* may be the most outrageous thing you could ever imagine. So, let's look at the trunk of a tree as an example: Because its stature is upright, similar to that of a human, what you'll see is a fatherlike identity in the tree, loving you more than your mother ever could. The love that comes from inanimate objects is much greater than the love your mom or dad tries to give you.

The explanation for this has already been mentioned: Love from the Father is *pure-love*, unfettered by stray thoughts that might be detected from mom or dad while giving you their love. For instance, mom is hugging and loving you with everything she has, but her love has been screened by many years of applications masking her pure-love; maybe from worrying, preoccupied with daily chores, or paying attention to somebody else. Anything that can interrupt pure-love will be detected by the child, making the love from mom or dad appear to be less important than the love coming from the presence of the Father. The love emanating from the Father, seen in objects of reality, is phenomenal by comparison—to say the very least!

Because it has already been established that the Father (dada) is God, you can now understand why so many people, unknowingly, use the term *God Loves You.* For some strange reason, these people seem to be obsessed with the idea that there is something about the origin of life that convinces them there is a creator that unconditionally loves them. And again, as ridiculous and outrageous as all this may seem, they are right!

God is Watching You

As the Father shows himself in objects of reality, he is also communicating all of his behavioral commands. In this way, it's like he is watching over you, making sure you are taken care of. One of the most prominent ways he does this is through the behavior of *love*. It should go without saying, that if he loves you, then he must be watching you.

Fall from Grace

The thought of the Father, as our origin, fades during early childhood, but the sense of grace is retained and interpreted within future applications (without direct identification of the Father). This sense of grace connects us to the Father through both mental and physical sensations—and although his visual experience may be lost, a slight residual sense of grace is still present.

When a person's perception of grace is challenged through intense concentration within life's applications, it can be progressively impaired and possibly, at older ages, totally lost. As this sense of grace is lost, the ability to effectively maintain physical functions may also be lost. During this process, some people find it difficult to walk, and talk, or even think right, as if they've lost the physical coordination and mental motivation for life. This can happen to children as well as adults.

Everything felt inside is possessive, while feelings outside are non-possessive. (This may also affect certain interpretations of grace.) When specific thoughts are expressed from within, they can interrupt outside feelings, and consequently become possessive, which sometimes causes a sense of "self-righteousness." But when interpreted outside, they are naturally non-possessive and not self-righteous.

Losing grace means that a person's actions have been so concentrated and possessed from within that the physical sensation and manner of 'flowing and loving thoughts' has faded.

Lent

During the process of submission, certain thoughts are surrendered that have already been imprinted to the memory. In this case, these are thoughts of possession, like owning a bicycle, a car, toys, or a house, and everything in the house.

But these things are not possessed by you when you are in a state of *Lent*. This means you lose the sense of possession of anything and everything, both in reality and inside your mind that you feel you possess. It's like they belong to someone else who is an authority over you, like the patriarch of your family (the Father).

For example: when Melina was a toddler, everything was given to her by mom and dad, and because they bought these things and even took care of them for her, she didn't feel like they belonged to her. In *Lent*, it's like mimicking the sense of being a little kid, which relieves you of having to take charge of all these possessions.

This taking charge of things is your sense of responsibility—not just for yourself, but for others as well. All these belongings and responsibilities add up in the memory and can confuse the mind into a sense of torment, leaving you feeling they are possessing you instead.

If nothing in life suggests that you possess or are in charge of anything at all means that you have submitted your possessive thoughts and are actually in a state of mind of *Lent*.

The Rapture: Cocooned

Seeing the Father is one thing, but meditating back before any sense of reality is like maintaining a conscious awareness of him without any sense of reality. It's sort of like being *cocooned:* wrapped up in a giant white blanket of love with a dominant Father. This is when contact with reality is lost and replaced by the pure consciousness of the Father. (This is also known as "The Ascension")

This first happened as a baby and on occasion, years later. It's like reality turned into a giant cocoon of the Father. Everything, in reality, disappeared leaving only me and my sense of ecstasy with the Father while temporarily suspended in this cocoon—sort of like backing out of reality right back into the womb. (Reality didn't disappear, it was only a memory illusion created in my mind.)

During this experience, the Father was seen centered as a prominent authority, broadcasting light around the womb, creating a brightening motherlike love. This is what I called the *white cocoon.* In this cocoon, the Father was not sitting on a white stone or throne with a crown as described in certain religious texts, and it wasn't Jesus. My analogy is that it was simply the memory of my real father and mother while I was being formed inside mom's womb.

Though I can't remember being born, I'd guess this is how I entered into this world: born from mom's womb still aware of the white cocoon; and then began to notice what appeared to be streams of colored light until they formed as objects of this new reality. It's like coming out of a dream-like state of being into a fatherlike reality. In my new environment, life began as a dream, but I soon learned how to make it real!

Giving-up Life

I get the strong feeling that this *rapture* is what Jesus was talking about when he said he went up and *"Sat on the right hand of God the Father Almighty."* This scenario suggests that he completely let go of his sense of reality. There comes a time in the cocoon when it's like holding onto life only by a thread. I can cut this *thread of life* at any time. But when I do, I will lose my sense of reality, yet still be conscious of the Father with all his elements of behavior, as well as the process of the forming of my life (like in the womb). But this may also happen during the process of dying—it's similar to the old saying, "meet your maker."

However, this 'giving up life' may not necessarily mean that I can't come back to life. In the case of Jesus, after he cut his thread of life, he did come back. He did so because there was no reason for him to die. He was probably in perfect health but realized he preferred the reality of the Father to the awful state of society, at that time. This coming back to the awareness of reality is known as being *born again.* (Some Christians use this term as a facsimile to describe the result of their submission because it's like a revival or feeling of being renewed or saved.)

Jesus obviously didn't die during this process of his Ascension, neither physically nor mentally. He simply went into the place in his mind where he was conscious of his creation, by the Father, and then came back out to the awareness of reality, retaining a sense of the Father as a Deity. (There may be a misconception that this only took place after his crucifixion. But this phenomenon more than likely happened even before he was known as a prophet, preaching in his later years. This *going up to see the Father* was his reason to begin preaching in the first place—to tell us about the presence of the Father.)

Woman Made from Man

The Bible tells a story, that a woman was made from the lung or bosom of a man. This sounds like a very interesting tale. But is it true?

While looking at the Father as a Deity in objects of reality, it is clear that his identity also contains the identity of a female (feminine). This identity is one of the behavioral elements that make up the fatherlike identity and is responsible for projecting the love of the Father into reality. A term often used to describe love is, *heart*. So, you could say, it's like the heart of the Father. The heart is located in the chest or lung area also referred to as the *bosom*.

Because the original behavioral elements of the Father were reversed—resulting in the *love* behavior as prominent—which is what made the female identity, this then set the stage for the creation of a new and separate being.

As mentioned earlier, the XY chromosome represents a father identity. Ironically, the X part appears to represent the love behavior of a female. Many animals, other than humans, are also under this same system of reproduction. This means that the female element X, at some time in the distant past (maybe nearer to the first life-forms on earth) was copied from the XY to create a new separate being: female (XX chromosome).

The foregoing scientific explanations appear to agree with the passage in the Bible that "woman was made from the bosom or lung of man." Although this idea is essentially correct, by examining the foregoing closer, and after studying biological history, we find this scenario did not begin with humans but with some species much earlier.

The Bible is somewhat flawed by calling it *man* rather than *the Father*. The physical identity of a man began with the Father, which is the spiritual identity from which the behavioral element of *love* (the prominent female identity) was taken.

God the Deliverer

My sense of this Father-deity tells me that he is sending me thoughts from my surroundings. And, even though I'm only somewhat aware of his presence inside, I am more entertained by his presence and behavioral elements emanating from objects of reality, as if these objects really do hold his spirit.

I'll guess that this experience appears to be similar to being formed in mom's womb, where I was aware of being put together by the Father taking charge and delivering all the parts to form my body. Then after I was born, I retained this same awareness. This is when I was under the impression that the Father was not only the deliverer and creator of all things in my new reality but constantly introduced new thoughts from reality in much the same way as he helped assemble me in the womb.

Throughout all my years, I have never heard anyone from any religious community say that "God is going." This is always referred to as, "God comes to you" or "God is the Deliverer."

Image of the Father

The Bible says that God created man and all manner of things in his image. For those who can remember the presence of Father, they'll see how easy this is to believe. But how this statement ever made it into the bible, I'll never know! Someone had to have remembered his presence as a Deity, way back even before the time of Jesus and Judaism.

Giving Thanks

Every time we say *grace* at the dinner table we are in essence, applying a prayer–ritual designed to get us in the mood for submission, by thanking the Lord–God with a feeling of gratification for everything he has given us. Everything in our environment was created or given to us by the Father. In his Divine presence, I am communicating with a Deity who is sending me information from my reality. After I accept this information and begin to process it, I am overcome with the feeling of love. This is the gratification stage of my communication with him. As a result of this gratified feeling, I am further overcome with a very common expression that we all know as *thank you.*

This idea of giving thanks may not be a social custom handed down through ancestry as much as it seems to be the result of a cycle of thought–communication with the Deity. If this is true, then it's easy to see how this social custom of giving thanks to the Lord–God grew from a universal, natural law of process. When you are aware of the Father giving you the love of life, you return the favor by submitting your feelings of gratification by saying, *thank you*—you have just completed a *cycle of thought* confirming your association with him. This is a natural phenomenon; I'd guess was around long before religion and does not have to be connected to religion to understand it.

The Soul

The soul is the foundation upon which all life is supported. So it should go without saying, that everybody has a soul. Consider the Genetic Memory as the soul, and that each person has a different design GM, making each person's personality unique. The Father represents the very inception of the soul; the controller of the GM and the origin-identity of life, itself.

Eternal Life

It appears that all life was born through the consciousness of the Father. Even though we can't always see him, his perpetual consciousness is what makes this day come alive. This sense of being alive will be flowing through hereditary lines for generations to come, to keep them alive. As long as we maintain a conscience for him, life will never die! This is the idea of *eternal life* that religions have been proposing for many generations.

But eternal life is also about death and dying. You know how to be born because all of the children in your ancestry were conceived before their parents died. Conversely, there is no way you can know anything about dying because none of the parents died before their children were conceived. If your dad had died before he conceived you, then you might know how to die. But because this does not exist in your genetic memory anywhere, you don't have any reference point from which to understand it, and therefore are unable to know anything about dying.

The only thing one might know about dying is going back to the white cocoon; back into a womb-like state of being. If this is what dying is or what takes place during the dying process, then you should know what it's like: it's like being born in reverse, backing out of the consciousness of reality right back into the consciousness of the Father.

It's easy to see from this scenario how the presence of the Father represents eternal life for every person, animal, or thing that has existed, and will exist for as long as new creations are as perpetual as the Father's presence has proven to be over the eons of time.

Religious Similarities

Mentioned here, are only several of many religious terms that could be applied as similar to the perspective of these notes, through the presence of the Father: *The Church; The Holy Ghost; Children of God; God Loves You; God is Watching You; Fall from Grace; Lent; The Rapture; Giving-up Life; Woman Made from Man; God the Deliverer; Image of the Father; Giving Thanks; The Soul; Eternal Life;* and the list goes on and on. These religious sayings can't be ignored because they are so strikingly similar to the experience children realize every day. In fact, they are so similar I am going to replace the word *similar* with the word *identical.*

If you have any reservations about how religion came to be, then all you have to do is remember your childhood experiences in the presence of the Father. This is the only way you'll get a handle on what these religious terms are about and how religion has set a standard of behavior for all people to follow—not just personally through the love of family, but also through the laws that have been enacted by every governmental institution worldwide.

Keeping It Alive

Though religions can't directly see this, they are trying to remind us of the Father's presence without understanding what is really taking place. There are times when it can be difficult to remember any single thought unless prompted to do so. We must be reminded, or else it might remain entombed in memory forever.

After a memory is lost, it seems as if there is no way of getting it back. Memory is the only thing keeping this thought alive. It would be nice if there were other methods of retrieving this thought of the Father; maybe one of the best ways to accomplish this is to talk to children about it directly because they are the ones doing it.

The only reason we'd even think that a father-like Divine Presence exists as what we call God, is that someone remembered and told somebody else, who wrote it down, keeping the idea alive over the annals of time. This one, simple act of documenting memories is what helped develop religion into what we know it today.

Religions all over the world, whether they be Christian, Judaism, Islam, or others, are attempting to make people believe that some sort of supreme-being exists as our salvation in life and are keeping that belief alive until the time comes when we will know for sure that the "presence of the Father" as a Deity is our one-and-only true God.

The Missing Link

These notes tell of the presence of a Father-deity that fits the description of what religious organizations call God and the Divine Presence. But understanding God should not be dependent upon religious belief alone. What is missing from the religious experience is how the understanding of God is directed up through the human social conscious and seen in reality as a fatherly Deity. That little four-letter word *dada*, nestled at the confluence of Religion and Atheism, is the *Missing Link* between belief and reality. If you could tap into your sense of a Deity, you'd find that *Belief in God* is replaced by a *Reality of God*

6
Talking to Kids

I know what you're thinking; kids are just looking for their daddy (parent). But let's look around this for a minute and see if we can't find another reason.

It's not right for children to limit themselves to just one perspective of understanding the Father's presence. If you can understand this as multipurpose, you might go looking for your daddy-parent because the identity is similar. But this doesn't excuse the fact that kids won't find explicit instructions coming from the Father to do this. When kids turn away from their human father and pay attention to the Father identity they see emanating from objects of their immediate surroundings, they should sense specific commands about their origin instead.

Who cares if you want to think that this thing called *dada* is for finding your daddy? In the presence of the Father, Melina and I learned something of more value: an appreciation for all things, by a very familiar, patriarch-like Divine being showing off a few basic behavioral principles. And the more we became familiar with these, the more enlightened we were.

Over the ages of time, if we all had been told that dada was God, would we have believed it as much as we believe—what we have been told by our parents—that it's just little kids who want their daddy parent? Parents should understand the impact this experience of the Father's presence might have throughout the rest of their child's life.

A Right to Know

Everyone has a right to know the truth about their origin. But at the same time, for some children, especially those who have already grown up into social conformity, this subject may not be such a fun thing to learn. They may have difficulty accepting this in competition with conformist standards at school, church, and other socially structured institutions. Nonetheless, somebody should let them know what the Father is all about so they will understand more about it before they've grown too far into social conformity.

Once known, maybe this memory of his presence won't spread out into society for many years if it happens at all. But until then, each one of us should at least have the right to know "what is going on."

Proof through Memory

What if airplanes weren't known to exist because nobody took pictures and archived them? So how do I prove dada (the presence of the Father) really exists? Well, I took mental pictures of him and stored them in my memory—they're in your memory too. These notes are trying to get them out where they can be seen and remembered. It might also help if some other people were involved in this process.

Let's look back to early childhood years... Some people have good memories of childhood, but others may not be able to remember any further back than age five, making the memory of the Father's presence almost impossible. In this case, you don't have to believe what all this is saying, but you might understand the truth about his presence, by observing your kids when they walk up to a swing or sandbox, then grab it and say, *daddy*. Here is a situation that warrants further investigation on behalf of the parents, but this still may not be enough proof!

The First Word

Children don't always call for their daddy. Sometimes it's mommy! But *mommy* is never used as an 'object of sense' in the same way as *daddy* (the Father). In this case of an identity seen in things, you don't ever hear them call things, *mommy*, *sissy*, or *Auntie Em*, it's always *daddy*.

This may be first realized when a baby is lying on his back in the crib. Blood flows from the front to the back of the brain, slowing activity in the conscious memory area. This is when the acquired-thoughts become less active, allowing the original genetic-thought of the Father to be recognized. In response to this action, the child adds another action by making the sound of *da*; and then will be more exclamatory and repeat the *da* like, *da–da*; and when put together quickly, it sounds like *dada*.

When you hear an infant say, *da* or *dada*, he or she isn't just practicing the first identifiable word in life just because it's cool, these kids, in fact, really do see things that appear to look like a father and then imprint this vision to the memory. It's sort of like experiencing a mirror image of the most prominent thing they know. This is a child's first step into intelligent recognition of how to respond to a total environment while also learning to grow within it. This is something parents will have to prove to themselves and come to terms with, by talking with their children to learn what they have to say about their experiences in the Father's presence.

Myth or Memory

I would like to make clear that the total experience of *daddy*, seen in objects of reality, is not the same as recognizing the human parent. If the thought of the male parent came first—to prompt the vision of the Father as a Deity—then I could understand the direct association. But, as memory serves me, the Father was directly identified in things without any connection to my daddy-parent. This is a stand-alone experience, excluding the thought of the male parent, and for that matter, both parents.

When children don't look to their daddy-parent but turn around and look to where the thought is coming from, any acknowledgment of the parent goes away, and they surprisingly discover something quite different: their true origin of life! They will see specific behaviors being presented to them by a fatherlike identity seen as a ghost in objects of their reality. This is their direct proof that dada is a Deity-like God much more than just an instruction to *go find your daddy*.

At first glance, and through my memory of going through these experiences as a child, it almost seems that looking for my human father was nothing short of a myth. However, it should go without saying, that because the identity of dada is basically the same, the child will eventually learn to match the dada identity, as seen in reality, with that of the human father, by default. This is obviously how the parent got tagged with the named–identity of *daddy*.

Seen not Heard

Kids often may not say anything while in the presence of the Father, making it difficult to know what they are seeing and experiencing at such time. If you think your son or daughter has never seen the Father's presence, think again! I can remember times when I didn't say anything while in his presence.

It may be possible that your children never verbalized this, but it doesn't mean that the Father's presence wasn't there. Sometimes it's no different than watching them going about life in an ordinary manner—and you can't tell. But at other times you can tell because you can see it in their eyes. If your toddler gets big eyes and looks intently at objects with great joy, this might suggest the appearance of dada.

Can't Talk Back

Here is an example: Now it's time to talk to your one- and two-year-old children and explain to them that this thing they call *daddy* is really the Father and that he is the intuitive precursor to everything they will experience in their future; and that when they reach age five, they might lose their ability to experience his presence again, and begin to experience severe problems coping with life as a result.

Can you see the problem here? It should be obvious what's happening! The difficulty arises when you can't tell children of one or two-years of age anything about this—how can they respond when they haven't fully developed a colloquial language yet? And, as they grow, it may become even more difficult because the Father's presence is less frequent, and therefore, harder to catch them in the act of these experiences.

It almost seems to be an oversight or glitch in the human design that we are allowed to develop through infancy without retaining any conscious knowledge of the Father, solely because we can't communicate.

One important focus of this book is to break the language barrier at an early age so parents can communicate with their kids while they are in the presence of the Father—and as a result, popularize this *graceful reality* so they will grow up carrying this memory throughout their entire lives.

Generation Gap

The problem of a communication gap (often referred to as a generation gap) exists between parents and their kids. If both parents were mirrored more as 'the manner of the Father' in their nature, they would be closer to their kids. Growing pains might be more easily resolved or even eliminated by the Father's influence within the family before their children grow up. This would especially apply to the tumultuous teen years when social problems begin to take root in their conscience.

It's difficult to approach kids about this because they might not want to talk to someone who isn't doing the same thing they are. For example, parents don't have sex with their kids, so why should they talk to them about it? Parents aren't experiencing this father identity, so why should they talk to their kids about it? Kids don't recognize any of this because parents never talk about it. When we were kids, nobody gave us any reason to remember, so we didn't!

If we can teach children all over the world how to speak a language and work mathematical problems, we surely must be able to teach them about the memory of their experiences in the presence of the Father and what it means for their overall well-being.

Nobody's Talking

The Father is stuck inside the memory and can't get out by himself. He needs help! By teaching kids, the fine art of 'belief and worship' or other kinds of rituals to get this out, kids might become confused.

This is especially true for children who are just beginning to learn how to speak. Maybe the best way to explain the reason for a ritual is simply to talk to them about their experience with the Father's presence and how they came to realize it. Instantly, this is intellectually out in the open for all to understand.

Isn't it strange that millions of children see the presence of the Father every day, and millions upon millions of adults don't understand it!

Power to Communicate

Learning about the Father's divine presence, as common among all children, could be the greatest cause for their future. But for this to be properly taught, it needs to be passed back-and-forth over a long period of time.

Because all of us were born with the love of the Father, which delivers our basic, instinct to communicate, children should be encouraged to share their sense of life from within the *aura of the divine*, well-knowing the Father's presence is right behind it. And through this powerful act of communication children will be more likely to establish camaraderie with one another.

Shame and Conformity

Through the trials of growing up, children sort of train themselves to be ashamed of things to which they can't conform, which floods them with inhibitions for the remainder of life (SCS). And, because no one teaches them to conform to the love of life that the Father shows, this consequently becomes the greatest shame of all. I can't see how parents could properly train their kids not to be ashamed of their inability to conform when they, themselves, haven't been properly trained to understand his Divine Presence.

Fear of the Deity

Children become afraid of this live-being Deity presence during the night, usually while alone. We were brought up not being told why we were afraid of this. Even as grown adults this can still be a scary thing to grasp. Nonetheless, now that it's out in the open and you've become familiar with it, there is no longer any reason to be afraid of knowing the Father's presence at night.

Children have unconsciously learned to carry this nighttime fear with them throughout their entire lives. It is so important that parents openly talk to their children and friends about this fear. Being afraid of our original identity has silently festered within each person as a negative consequence of life. One can only wonder how much this has affected children after they have grown into adults.

If your children become scared at night and swear there is someone in the room with them, you can tell them: there is nothing to fear, it won't hurt you; it's more than likely just the presence of the Father who loves you during the day.

It's almost tragic that this fear consequently forces children to be deprived of the very thing they've loved and cherished the most. Other than making sure your kids remember their wonderful experience with the Father, their fear of him may well be one of the most important messages you could ever give them to remember.

Family Values

The family doesn't recognize the Father because he is like an individual experience that precedes the idea of a family. Each family member, collectively, creates the sense of a family from personal experiences in the presence of the Father. This, in turn, creates a unique sense about the family that identifies it as one cooperative unit. Unfortunately, a family can't talk about any of this if the Father has never been properly identified.

An entire family needs to get together and understand this more clearly to guarantee the idea of collective independence for each family member while at home with the Divine Presence. Until this is done, the family will have no sense of what their children are really about or how all this works in harmony to create well-formed oriented values that give the family an *aura of the Divine* sense about itself.

Drugs and Kids

By the time kids become teens, they have learned thought concentration processes, which cause the senses to fade, by preempting the sensing thoughts prominently held in recognition of the Father. And since hallucinogenic drugs have been used by adults in order to awaken the Divine Presence, it is only natural that kids would also try to use them as a means to rediscover this great natural and original sense of life.

Ideally, kids should be brought up in a favorable environment where they'll feel the freedom to occasionally socialize through the *aura of the Divine* as their primary guide away from drugs. And, because they will already be familiar with this experience, they won't have to try to mimic this by using drugs.

A Birthright

Children are self-taught to proclaim themselves as individual deities through their intimate experiences with the Father. So, it seems ridiculous to think you can teach something to someone who already knows more about the subject than you. For this reason, parents can't teach these intimate experiences to kids without any knowledge of what is going on in his Divine presence. But if they know it exists, they can at least teach them to keep their memory of him alive in everything they learn and do—I often wonder what the outcome would be like.

After kids have grown into adulthood and have experienced problems from social pressures, they may need to look back to their experiences of the Father's presence as a point of salvation. In this respect, his memory should not be looked at as a religion, but as a *birthright* that should be taught at an early age. Children should have the opportunity to learn from the sensuality of their true origin, of which they have been deprived, by conforming to the many regimented, and at times, thought-provoking ideas of society.

It is just as important to nurture a child's sense of the Divine Presence as it is to clothe, shelter, and feed him. It is ultimately up to the parents to give their children a sense of origin to carry with them for life.

Adult, Not Baby

We grew up dragging the memory of baby identification along with us rather than the adult identity of the Father we learned as children. This identity is not baby-like, and not an "inner child," but an alive, cool and confident adult identity. It should go without saying that children ought to be told that this identity is what makes them grow up into adults—because if they can remember the presence of the Father, they should already know this.

Videos and Games

Because toddlers haven't developed a language yet, they are not able to communicate with you when they are showing off their experiences in the Father's presence. So, here are some things you can do to get your kids to remember this great experience, and maybe at the same time prove to yourself that a Father-deity, indeed does exist...

If you don't have a video camera, get one! Catching your toddler on video while in the presence of the Father should prove the existence of this experience as well as aid memory recall. And when your children reach age four or five and have learned to speak and communicate but have lost this memory, this is time to break out the video. You now have the perfect opportunity to interact and ask them about this experience to see what they have to say about it.

A game many parents will play with their child is, *go find daddy*. (Be sure to have your video cam ready for this one.) When both parents are present, they might observe their son going around grabbing things and calling them *dada*. The mother will see this and try to train her toddler to find his daddy-parent by saying, *go find daddy*. More than likely, if the mom or dad doesn't say anything to entice the child into going for the daddy-parent, he will go for inanimate objects like the coffee table or the chair, or maybe even crawl up onto dad's lap and grab for the lamp. Kids will usually ignore their human father during a session with dada because the magnitude of the Father's presence is so much greater.

This little game of *go find daddy* has resulted in children having learned that their human father is really dada because their parents have trained them to believe it.

An inverse strategy can be applied for getting your children to remember the Father's presence: Instead of giving them the notion that their human daddy is dada—because the two identities are similar—the daddy-parent identity is used to remember the presence of the Father, not vice-versa.

It also might be a good idea, at this time, to educate the child so he or she can distinguish the difference between a father parent and the dada experience with the Father: call the parent *daddy* and the Father *dada*.

Parents' Primary Obligation

It should be a parent's job to appropriately place the memory of the Father's presence in a child's active thought processes along with all other learning activities. But it would not be right to say things that might convince your child to understand something that could be confusing. It's like giving your child false information, for example: *Now you really didn't see dada in that tree, did you?* This will complicate the child's understanding of his true sense of origin.

Also, it may not be a good idea to confuse your own religious beliefs with the presence of the Father when you talk to your kids. Many of us traditionally have taught our children, as well as ourselves, religious methods that use mystical terms. We've never directly talked to our kids about their obligation to learn about the origin of their identity, so the real, true message was never revealed. This should be understood as more of a natural function of human development than a religious belief.

Our children will be the ones responsible for initiating the awareness of this Divine Presence in society. If children could only remember their experiences of being in the presence of the Father, it might very well affect their future decision-making through productive social behavior. This will never happen unless children are taught to "put on" a state of mind to continuously practice their association with him. If we can teach our kids to behave with a sense of order for society, then we most certainly should be able to get them to remember experiences connected to their origin of life.

7

Rationalizing It

*You won't know any of this until
you've seen it in action and remembered.*

Bonding with the Father

I was born with both a mom and a dad inside me, represented as individual parts of my ancestral heredity line. While developing in my mother's womb, I imagine that I imprinted the manner of her mother-identity through awareness of her physical nature. So, after I was born, I already had a physical bond with my mother, but no sense of bonding with a physical father. It seems that I would naturally go looking for my father (human parent) to bond with soon after birth. (This has been the accepted rationale for as long as I have known.)

But this doesn't excuse the fact that this father, who I was supposed to be looking for as my human parent, very prominently showed up as a Deity emanating from objects of reality instead. This makes sense because babies could have difficulty sensing the 'origin father-identity' in the human parent. This is because his natural identity is masked through years of a social conformity type of personality emanating from him.

In the very beginning, my human father was just another ordinary object of reality, but one that I did not focus on as much—he was just one of many.

After birth, the mother is mostly responsible for nurturing the baby's physical well-being. But neither parent can adequately nurture the baby's thought processes, especially concerning his or her surroundings. So, this is left up to the Father to teach the child how to respond to objects of reality. A human father can't do this for a baby who has not yet learned how to communicate—the baby will need some help doing this. So, bonding directly with things seen in reality through the sense of the Father happens by default. To clarify all this: the baby retains a familiar physical motherlike identity; then after some time, as the brain becomes aware of reality, the fatherlike identity activates the brain thought processes, thus prompting the baby to respond, by calling things *dada*. This means that the mother is the *physical deliverer*, and the Father is the *thought activator*.

Throughout millions of years of life evolution, you'd think that human children, by now, would have developed a basic instinct to reach for their human parent after birth. But they don't! The Father identity from within the genetic memory connects with objects of reality outside. This creates a condition that polarizes the baby's overall sense of being, establishing a very close bond between the baby and the Father, both sharing a very special relationship through reality. Being that the baby's focus of attention to life is from within this sense of polarity, the thought of the human father is preempted as a result, making him less important.

Conception and Messiah

It is through my perspective that anyone who sees the presence of the Father is also experiencing the point of that person's very beginning; sort of like a giant spark of love that ignites the first sense of being alive. So, each time the Father appears—which could be many times during childhood—the child is, in essence, connecting that spark of his or her conception with physical reality. This results in a feeling of being reborn and, at least temporarily, "saved" from an ill sense of social conformity.

Further understanding also reveals that a repetition of this occurrence could be seen as a practice in realizing a *Messiah* or savior. The prophecy of the coming of a Messiah in the form of 'one person only' might be viewed as a misnomer ("old wives' tale"). A more realistic sense of a Messiah is when each person reconnects with the Father as a Deity in reality. This means that many people, collectively, might very well make up the body of the Messiah. It almost should go without saying that—until everyone can learn to experience the presence of the Father regularly—there may never be a Messiah; for this is the true inner realization of the origin of us all! [This is the *extreme perspective* mentioned at the very beginning of this book.]

The Burning Heart

Making complete rational sense of this phenomenon of the Father's presence requires revealing a detailed description of what a child is going through during this process...

To bond with the Father, I must go thru the heart. (From this viewpoint, the heart is like a mother, *delivering* his presence.) I begin within the sense of the *aura of the Divine* about my immediate surroundings; then, through a high degree of humility and natural meditation, I will soon be overcome by a feeling of inner-peace sometimes accompanied by a warm or even burning sensation in the heart.

This burning sensation is the *tipping point* of humility when I realize I can choose to either stay connected to a social conformist conscious or surrender it.

There are two opposing perspectives that will relieve this burning sensation:

1. Continue to meditate and surrender very deeply within the inner-peace and burning heart. This takes me back toward my sense of origin, and the burning sensation in the heart will disappear, replaced by a surprise: *the presence of the Father.* (A visual identity literally pops out of the woodwork.)

2. Disregarding surrender by actively conforming to social situations with other people or things, here and now, makes the burning in the heart disappear. If, however, I happen to be in the Father's presence, social conformity will also cause his presence to disappear, returning me to an after-sense: the *aura of the Divine.*

Melina notes: This burning heart may not always be present in babies and toddlers, because the burning sensation is caused by holding on to conformist thoughts before they are released. The older you are, the more thoughts you'll have to hold on to, and therefore, the burning becomes more noticeable.

Revisiting the White Cocoon

As described earlier, this cocoon's character was a white feminine envelope of love with a masculine identity appearing as the focal point of my attention—sort of like a king on a throne with power of authority over me. After birth, I didn't like my new physical reality and wanted to return to the comfort and love of the womb. (Of course, I didn't physically crawl back inside because this was only my memory; a mental vision of what it was like while being formed inside mom's womb.) I can only imagine that I experienced this phenomenon many times during my first week or so of life until I could trust that the physical environment outside of the womb was not going to hurt me. Eventually I needed more help getting oriented to my new reality when not envisioning the white cocoon... This is when the white cocoon of feminine love was transformed into objects of reality and the dominate Father showed himself as a *thought sense* and main focus in one of the objects, which I called *dada*, giving me comfort and joy, and confidence learning how to interact with my new reality. The Father helped me through this each time I returned to this *mental cocoon*. This whole process was like being reborn. I wonder how many others have experienced this same phenomenon. I would take a guess that the answer is, *everyone*.

Through each returning visit, I would fixate on the masculine identity more than the feminine. If I had fixated more on the feminine, I wonder if I would have been inclined to take on a sense of female sexual identity in life and might grow up with a sense of gender opposite that of my male physical anatomy.

Outside the Bubble

I can only imagine that while in my mother's womb I was surrounded by a lot of flesh and fluid, but after some time I was overcome with a strong sense that there was something outside of this bubble of a womb I was in—like the thing that created me. I wanted to get out and find out what is going on. This was the point in my life when I first realized that I am naturally energized with the sense to explore and discover.

After birth, I carried this same sense of creation into reality, but now see a new womb with all kinds of neat things like, pillows, furniture, trees, dogs and cats, and a blue sky that fills with stars at night. These visions serve as entertainment within my new reality; an entertainment that was missing in mom's womb. Yet, here in this beautiful reality on earth, there are times when I look up at the sky and say, *I know there is something out there*—sensing there is something outside the reality of earth, in outer space. I want to find out what is outside this bubble of atmosphere here on earth. For some strange reason, I have a strong feeling that my creator, who is also responsible for my well-being, is out there somewhere.

If we humans were to discover and understand the entire universe as much as we understand about life here on earth, we would probably say, *there is something out there, beyond the universe that we can't see.* We might get a strong sense that our creator, as well as the answer to all of our problems, lies somewhere in the black unknown beyond our known universe.

We seem to be constantly searching for the answers to life, hoping that all the problems that have plagued us since the beginning of time will be resolved as soon as we can make direct contact with our origin. But as much as we have tried over the ages of time, this contact has been unseen and unheard-of....

Wait a minute...It is seen, and it is heard, by millions of kids every day trying to get adults to recognize what they are experiencing while in the presence of the Father. Even though it appears that the origin of life did begin somewhere in outer space, the quest to begin understanding this is right before our very eyes, right here inside the bubble of earth.

Realizing God

How did we ever come to realize there is a God? Because you are reading this book, you should already know the answer. But let's explore this again, by looking back into our past...

It would seem that someone or some group of people—maybe the very first human beings—understood this phenomenon of the presence of the Father and passed it down through the ages of time. If these people were here today, one might describe it like this:

"Genetic energy holds the presence of a fatherlike identity within my conscious. There is also fatherlike genetic energy in things of reality that draws the energy from within my conscious out into my surroundings. This produces a social sense for my reality that makes everything seem to come alive with the identity of a father."

It might also be said like this: "There is a fatherlike memory inside me that appears in objects of reality as a live-being Deity—very similar to a person—though, without human form. A polarity between my Father memory and the objects creates my alive sense of reality. This also establishes a very close bond between the outside Father-deity and me, where we both share a very special kind of loving relationship within my new reality. It's a communication between us that suggests that this Deity is not only the originator of all things in reality but the origin of myself, as well. Imagine a Deity-father introducing you to things in reality for the very first time, as if he owned or created all these things himself. Merging the two thoughts, *the presence of the Father as a Deity* and *the creator of all things* equal what we call *God*."

<u>But why is it called God?</u>

The word *God* may have many interpretations that have been passed down through the ages of time. But we don't want to get into a history lesson that we can't prove. Instead, we'll use modern language and the actual experience of the Father's presence. To explain this, let's create a three-letter acronym:

The Father is: The *Grandest* thing you can ever imagine + the *Oldest* thing in existence + poses in reality exactly like a *Deity* that is described by religions all over the world = **G**rand **O**ld **D**eity (GOD).

Going Back Salvation

As adults, in the present time, we'll probably never be able to go back to living a life in direct contact with the Father regularly and perhaps shouldn't even try. The real focus here is not for our self-serving salvation through belief, but once his presence is realized, simply talk to each other about the memory so it will grow in popularity.

This seems more like memory-salvation than ritual-salvation. It's pretty darn simple stuff. You don't need a high degree of education or worship through religion to understand this. Even though these notes are proposing to make a radical adjustment to society for all time, knowing who we are and where we come from sure makes a lot of sense for a society trying to evolve into something greater than it is now.

As we continue on our current paths through life as adults, our sense of aliveness can fade. Yet, if we ever wanted to go back to experiencing the presence of the Father, as we turn and move further back toward him, we'd find that the closer we come, the more a personal identification will come alive. Moreover, this creates a complication of having to remove objects of conformity and shame. This is a huge obstacle that leads us into a state of mind known as *humility*—this is sort of like a *stumbling block* in reverse.

For any adult to realize pure self-salvation enlightenment, they would have to break the barrier of years of *social conformity*, *shame through conformity syndrome*, and a *mothering identity*, of which I believe most adults, will have little chance of doing.

Nevertheless, total enlightenment is perhaps best resolved by each child maintaining a close connection to the origin, in association with others, as a continuous quest to be carried up into adulthood and passed on to future generations.

Throughout the recorded history of civilization, this rediscovery of a reality of the Father's Divine Presence has never been adequately accomplished—although it might have been attempted several times—each attempt has produced less than satisfactory results, for society at large, to truly understand what is going on.

The Glitch

This book is asking over and over, *why do we lose this memory and forget so completely?* It very well may be that we were designed, not to look or conform to the Father, but to turn away and look to creating things in society, by using the basic commands that he set for us while in his presence. This looks like the best reason because this is what we all have done! If we were to go back, could we still create and advance life? As mentioned earlier, the answer to this may be positive, but at the same time, still somewhat unclear.

If it were not in the original design of human beings to have this memory loss, then it appears that forgetting the presence of the Father may very well be a glitch in the human design.

Familiar Conformity

Progressive thought processes such as *popularization*, *active*, and *reactive*, are necessary thought patterns of a growing human being. But oftentimes action amongst these thoughts will develop confusion, causing severe social problems.

If we were to rationalize all thought processes down to one formula to resolve all problems, it might be termed *familiar conformity*. The process of familiar conformity repeats itself many times during one's lifetime, acting as a foundation for future conformity standards...

The more you love, the more love will work you; the more you hate, the more hate will work you; the more problems you work, the more they will work you; and the more you become familiar with the Father's Divine Presence, the more he will bond with you. When we are familiar with something, it is comforting; and we are more inclined to repeat what is comfortable.

We instinctively use this foregoing scenario during the process of conformity. And, if we get used to imprinting what is most familiar at an early age, then we can continue to build upon that familiarity throughout our entire lives. Being familiar with the Divine Presence would have to become a preemptive conformist issue in the face of all other social conformity for it to take root as a perpetual conscious foundation for all future social activities.

Using this as a lesson, we don't often affect change or advance in life by working with things we can't see. But in this case—through a conscious of the Father memory (something that is seen)—we might find we'd be even more able to resolve many more of our social and physical problems as a result.

Genetics

It is so easy to lose awareness of the Divine Presence to response-thoughts, conformity, and fear. If this has been going on since the beginning of time, then it only makes sense that maybe we have genetically programmed ourselves to use these events as devices to block thoughts of our origin. It therefore might take many generations to learn how to recondition and coordinate our consciousness of the Divine with social standards we use for work and play in everyday life.

Trust/Mistrust

Melina observed that the more a child exhibits a sense of origin, the more other children will be inclined to establish a firm base of camaraderie. At this point, it should go without saying that every person, deep down inside, recognizes the manner of the Father as their origin, which they can identify as a sense of sameness in others. This scenario creates a very comforting thought known as *trust*.

When I mistrust others, it does not necessarily mean that I don't like them, it's just that I feel my personal identification is being threatened. In other words, by mistrusting, I am trying to protect my fatherlike identity from shame. But sometimes this can have a reciprocal effect that urges me to surrender the shame, which helps open a channel of awareness of the *aura of the Divine*, which could ultimately lead a path directly to the presence of the Father.

The Natural Internet: Prayer Theory

Most of us refer to prayer as a religious act. But it is not religious at all, because prayer is, in essence, communication with everything that exists. This means that we are communicating with something, somewhere, at all times. Even if that something is just sitting around in one place looking out at the trees and flowers in the back yard, life itself is realized as the prayer!

As mentioned before, *communication* is *love*. Therefore, the more you love the more your prayers should come true. And, because we all love anyway, at least a little bit, prayers (the things we want) will either come true or not, regardless of how much we love. It's only when the basic element of love is concentrated through meditation that it seems like a miracle when prayers do come true.

Is this a figment of the imagination, or does raising the sense of love have any effect on prayer? Love may affect prayer if, what is desired is a relationship with other people. An old saying is, *"The more you love, the more you will be loved."* In this way, your prayers may have a better chance of being answered because you have opened a nice big communication channel that others can easily recognize and trust. Most people have no problem trusting those who love!

If our *love* is communication, then how are prayers communicated? This is somewhat more complicated, so we'll have to look at it technically, for instance: it's like mailing a request for something that you want or need; only instead of using the Post Office, you are going to use your sense of ESP to send signals—like radio waves—asking for what you want. You'll send a specific thought out into reality with your return address on it... And as an infinite number of thoughts communicate with one another in the ESP reality, any thought that matches yours will be delivered to your return address, and hopefully with a favorable answer.

To check this out further, it's similar to how a computer internet works, by sending and returning electronic signals. Computers were designed after the human design that uses the *natural internet*, and maybe all other species of animals and all things throughout the universe, as well.

If this is what prayer is, then how did it get into religion? The answer is simple: When a request for something is answered, it is delivered by the Father. The Father is my operating system, like a computer OS, so every thought that comes in is checked in by him and tagged with a fatherlike identity. The phrase *"The Father is the Deliverer"* is a religious term meaning *God the Father delivers the commands of life.*

Hide-and-Seek

Religions have organized, for our benefit, the ultimate game of *hide-and-seek* with our origin, making belief in a God difficult, at best. To resolve this inconsistency, it's not how we believe, but that we actually "realize" what it is we are trying to believe in. Everyone did this dada thing the same and got their education through his elements of behavior. This taught each one of us how to conduct ourselves in life before we ever knew anything about religion.

When I get a sense of the *aura of the Divine* about reality associated with the origin, I might first think of this as a religious experience. But if there were no religion, would I relate this aura of reality directly to my origin of life, or not? Religion just took this idea and made it a big deal, by creating ritual-worship!

If all religion were to disappear, would we still pay a certain degree of respect to our sense of origin in the same way as we pay to parents who brought us into this world and raised us?

Submission and Prayer

There is a need to submit to the Father, which is a natural act of human behavior built into the sensual social system. It's a necessary function for maintaining all the thoughts created through him.

When something traumatic happens, for example, a serious accident, illness, the death of a loved one, or extreme embarrassment, you'll give up some conscious thoughts, leaving only that of the Father and any other necessary thoughts of function that satisfy with a feeling of inner peace. This is the process of submission, which is often referred to as surrender.

Prayer is two-sided: it changes your mind about how to go about accomplishing something. As an example, you can pray that your mother will not die after an accident, and in such case your prayer will do one of two things: it will either change your mind about how to help her or change your mind forcing you to surrender your prayer, resulting in submission. This is when you give up trying and, if you are religious, *"Let God do the praying for you."*

Surrender makes me feel better! And through ESP communication, I believe that all things around me will conform to my feelings when I broadcast my 'submission of feeling' into reality. I don't know if this works in cases of severe trauma, but if I can make someone feel better through submission, then hopefully, this will make them feel better. The better you feel overall, the better your chances are of recovery.

We'll often think of this feeling of submission as if it is religious, and customarily refer to it by religious names and icons such as *"feeling Jesus"* or *"Godhead."* When people pray to God, more than likely, all they are doing is attempting to submit to their origin. Prayer is nothing more than an act of inducing submission to make contact with the thoughts of the Father, which are constantly flowing through each one of us.

It should go without saying that the process of praying is a random act; meaning that once you are cut off from your direct association with the Father, it appears the only way to reconnect with him is through prayer.

But this poses a problem. The point where you severed his memory is like a screen through which you can't see—so you'd have to go through this screen. It's like shooting at something you know is there, yet, when many of the shots don't hit the target, it then becomes a *try*—like shooting at something in the dark or gambling—both of which are dependent on chance.

If we could train children at an early age to remember the presence of the Father, they might just be able to create a continuous open channel of thought pointed directly toward him. This channel would then parallel all activities throughout their lives, making this process of prayer-meditation more natural and effective.

There is one more phenomenal twist of fate... If you understand all this, then you should be aware that this channel is, and always has been, right in front of us—we just have to learn how to clear a path through it.

A Sense of Timeline

I can't live in past or future times, but only here in the present, within the moment. I can, however, be aware of the past and future while still conscious of being in the present time.

The past and future are what holds the feeling of being alive through the *motion of time*. Living for each moment of entertainment, by maintaining a conscious for things to come, is what keeps the conscious happy and moving forward along the timeline of life. This is because entertainment, itself, is a process of time that takes place in the present. If I lose this sense of the timeline, I am condemned to be alienated and isolated from others. This isolation can take place through deep meditation and while in the deep state of rapture; this is when all active communication and entertainment from reality becomes lost in time.

Actively communicating a love of life through the sense and manner of the Father is what stimulates the timeline. Even though the experience of the presence of the Father is far within the moment, I will always find a compelling reason to continue pursuing life, by being entertained from within the *aura of the Divine*.

Certain events may not be held in a future time, but instead, take place in the present. For instance: *picking up a cup and walking into another room*; to do this, I would have to have learned a process to follow that will take place *here and now*. This process becomes the *present timeline*, not a *future timeline*. So, the present timeline can be defined as a place we call *here*, compared to the future timeline, which may be some distance from being "here." This is what is meant by *living in the present*.

Food for thought: We could debate whether there is a sense of *now* without any sense of past or future? But conversely, would there be a sense of past or future without a sense of *now*?

Love-Now

For the most part, this book is not proposing ritual methods or rules of salvation. Nonetheless, in this one-note and throughout the next chapter we'll explore a simple exercise of spiritual guidance.

Most of you should already know about peace of mind in a calm atmosphere of one's immediate environment, here and *now*. And because we are familiar with the presence of the Father, we should also know about *love*. Put these two together and you have, *Love-Now*: The Universal Love of all things.

Awareness of origin-thoughts of the genetic memory takes place in the conscious memory area of the brain. But when this area becomes clogged with too many acquired-thoughts, it slows the thought flow, diminishing the sense of the origin-thoughts. These thoughts of the origin are the fundamental thoughts of objects of reality originally introduced by the Father, here and now. *Love* is the natural mediation of life that unclogs the conscious memory area allowing new incoming *now* thoughts, from out, in reality, to flow through unrestricted, resulting in an overall sense of *Love-Now*.

While being loved by others, I am more conscious of the incoming love, like a meditation. Using this Love-Now method, I am training myself to pay attention to incoming thoughts to bypass reactionary outgoing thoughts that can alter the nature of the *pure-love* that is entering the conscious. If I do this right, love will flow through as an outgoing thought without being confused as a reaction to social conformity. The only response I will get is a feeling of gratification.

If I use objects of reality for the exchange of love, I won't need to love you directly because you will get it whether you want it or not. Look at it like this: Love is taken from all things in reality, just like while in the presence of the Father; this love is greater than the direct love I learned to take in from another person. This is *pure-love* that is literally, taken "off the wall." By taking responses from others *off the wall*, I have just filtered any social reactionary thoughts that can be interpreted as negative feelings—this is how *Love-Now* works.

In the presence of the Father, I love everything around me. This means that when I say, *I love you*, I will first have to love the Father, whose familiarity resides in objects of reality. By doing this I am putting the Father before you concerning the process of loving. In this way, I am loving you indirectly. But if I should decide to love you directly, then I am preempting the Father—this is not pure-love! However, there is an inverse happening that can take place: If I love you directly, this exchange of love can help broadcast the sense of love out to all things in the immediate environment creating an *aura of the Divine* sense of reality.

When you love, all the original behavior elements begin to assume their original values. If this love is deeply meditated over a very short period, you might, suddenly, find yourself in the presence of the Father (This mostly happens with children). Love-Now is an alternative approach to 'prayer through a belief in God,' and all you need to do is to *love* being here *now*. This is something that we all have in common, even though, at times, it may not seem like it! Love-Now is the closest you'll come to the presence of the Father because this is what the Father does. The Father is *authority*, *intellect*, and *order*. But what the Father does is *Love-Now*. And what the Father does is what you do in return—you've just completed a *cycle of love*! Want a prayer?

Love-Now is the ultimate prayer, and you don't have to go far to get it!

This single act of Love-Now is what produces the presence of the Father as he appears as a Deity in objects of reality. To truly understand how this works, I'll leave you with this one simple trick: How do you *Love-Now*?... You don't—*Now* will love you!

The First Step

Our very first step in life was overlooked, and therefore never firmly established; a step to develop common awareness among children about their sense of origin. And, because this first step was inadvertently omitted, we are left having to resort to ritual-salvation methodology in an attempt to regain this awareness.

Religions and other self-awareness organizations are only trying to get the Father out from inside, where his *aura of the Divine*, will help to generate self-healing, communication, and overall intelligent social progress.

Are we losing more and more of a sense of our natural order? Do we see this lack of order progressively growing around us? Are we breeding kids' day by day with a sense of social order that excludes this first step of understanding their origin?

The Bridge

The bridge to our natural social origin was, in effect, burned by an ancient civilization. To reconstruct this, we could begin by making a conscious effort to pursue it with a positive attitude. This reconstruction not only requires positive thinking but also dedication to a continuous challenge over a long period of time... People don't solely evolve—they make their reality evolve— which, in turn, makes them evolve.

This book is like a new bridge between our consciousness of society and recognition of our sense of origin. Yet, during the process of building this bridge, we'll find that the understanding of our original identity that has been missing is, and always has been, right in front of us. As adults, the only remaining bridge is our love of life and sense of grace—a bridge to the well-kept secret of our childhood experiences of the Father's Divine Presence.

8
Live-Meditation

Love-Now method of self-salvation

The main focus of this book is to bring the memory of our origin into common awareness. But after exploring the many notes covering this phenomenon, it's evident that, along with technical notes, it has become necessary to assist the memory recall by suggesting a simple, natural exercise without having to believe in a God or follow the many rules and ritual methods of worship in order to regain the enlightened conscious of our social origin.

Some believe that maintaining good health and economics will contribute to their salvation for survival. Nevertheless, one of the most effective methods of survival-salvation for every human being is to maintain a connection to their origin of life by practicing the Love-Now method of live-meditation.

Outside Sources

This trick for enlightenment was mentioned in the previous chapter: *You don't love— 'Now' will love you!* You might think this is ridiculous! How can a *Now* love me? Don't I generate my love from within?... Not exactly—and it's not so ridiculous! Ask yourself, do you generate your food and water from within? No, you don't! You get it from outside sources. So just like food, you get your love from outside sources too. Everything throughout reality is broadcasting love at all times, here within the moment. All I have to do is pay as much attention to the love coming in from all objects in reality as I do the objects, themselves. All objects, which also include live beings, communicate source-energy or Universal Love (U-Love) by passing it back and forth. When this happens, I realize that all things appear to love me—and at times, more than I could ever imagine—just like when I was a toddler! This is the Love-Now method of live-meditation.

First Acts of Life

As a baby, my first act was to *scream and cry* my way into birth, but my next was to *receive love* from all things surrounding me. All activities and learning experiences throughout life are based upon these two fundamental acts of sensing reality: one is the ecstasy of love, and the other is fearful and painful. Throughout my entire life, I have been Loving-Now by constantly being flooded with a universal type of love. However, this love oftentimes can be overshadowed by undesirable situations, similar to being born.

So, keeping this in mind, all I have to do is connect with reality, as I did as a baby, staying focused on the incoming U-love that seems to emit from all things around me. Only this time, if I am grown up, I won't act like a child but will experience reality as if I am closer to my original sense of life, and therefore sense reality more like a child...

Universal Love

Universal Love (U-Love) is the activity between two opposing forces that creates the sense of being alive as it emits from all things; and further creates an aura of love about reality known as the *aura of the Divine:* a family-like love. This love is continuously coming in from reality, even though we might not be aware of it. Love-Now is the awareness of this flow of thought as it invades and energizes the senses of the mind and body, thus creating physical activity responses that further complement other actions of reality in sort of a 'cycle of communication.'

Imagine love coming in from all things in reality, even from far away. This incoming love pushes out current internal thoughts, opening an 'exit gate' allowing bottled-up thoughts to leave the conscience, resulting in submission: a peaceful, internal feeling of gratification and love of life. This sense of love flows through me at different intervals or rate-of-speed depending upon how much thought I am currently holding in my conscious.

This meditation is like a light breeze: each moment is an individual segment as it gently blows by. Sometimes it is stronger and other times more subtle. But in either case, it is a continuous stream of thought, generating a *force of timeline*, producing a wide-awake feeling of being alive.

While enjoying this very familiar Universal Love flowing from all things, even from other people, you may often find yourself using it in certain *familiar conformity* situations: If I see all things as Loving-Now, then would I not be part of that love, as well? As an example, when I see my daughter discovering new things through her love of life, would I not also sense and feel that same love of life she is experiencing? (Monkey see...Monkey do!)

Sounds, sight, touch, smell, and taste of many things sensed from your surroundings can be either good or bad, but it's how they are communicated that will determine how you feel about them: If these physical senses are interpreted through the sense of Love-Now, you will enjoy them even though they may not always agree with you. If they are not sensed through Love-Now, you might become disgusted by them and carry around a set of bad feelings.

Process of Awareness

The idea of—being aware of incoming love from all things—should be recognized first, before any physical senses and actions take place, to achieve an enlightened sense of being. Physical senses will couple with and motivate the physical action of life only after they are energized by the love of the Father—which is Universal Love... *The U-Love activates senses, which in turn, motivates the action of life.*

Redirecting U-Love

Reality is constantly sending signals, teaching us the joy of life in everything we do through the Universal Love of the Father. Society, on the other hand, trains us in thought processing. Processing begins when attention from all things in your environment is redirected to one particular thing or object. This redirecting of incoming thought toward only one thing creates *outgoing* thought, which will often take on a *possessive* character.

Any thought you process belongs to you. All incoming thoughts of Universal Love belong to the Father and not to you—so they aren't possessed as they come in. (Sort of like the thoughts in your mind belong to you and not me.)

Being "possessed" from concentrating thought on one thing rather than all things, will have the effect of weakening the overall Love-Now experience, moving you further away from enlightenment.

Compassion and Passion

Compassion is when I take charge of the U-Love that comes in from all things, in reality, then direct that love toward one person or another living thing in a camaraderie manner.

Passion is directing love from all things toward one thing of action such as doing something like, skiing, biking, or even reading and writing.

In either case, the incoming U-Love is considered *non-possessive*, but processed and transformed into a *possessive* love as an outgoing thought. Occasionally this passionate type of love may encounter difficulties and result in unfavorable situations. Nevertheless, by maintaining U-Love consciousness, these difficulties will either appear opaque or not appear at all, since U-Love is not possessive.

This meditation of Universal Love seems to suggest that the *"love of all things is greater than the love of anyone!"*

Preempting Love of Life

Everything, in reality, is delivered by the Universal Love of the Father. Why then, would you allow someone to dominate your beautiful loving experience with a disagreeable behavior that takes up only a tiny percentage of all things in reality? This minuscule percentage can take over and cause extreme misery! Is it worth allowing this invasion of bad behavior when it can be preempted through Love-Now Meditation?

As an example: U-Love emits from all things including, physical structures, sounds, and even from human clothing. Any voice coming from another person that might seem objectionable could be preempted by maintaining awareness of U-Love, which is transmitted from clothing, skin, or sound. Also, the echo from other objects in your surrounding reality will help filter any bad attitudes coming from that person (Like taking bad thought "off the wall"). This exercise may not completely get rid of a nasty personality but will at least make it bearable enough to maintain a reasonable connection to the Divine through Love-Now meditation. When you are closer to the origin of your alive experience, then are you not closer to everybody else's too? And if luck prevails, maybe Love-Now will rub off on some rude person.

Attention vs. Intention

The attention of life begins by recognizing the Universal Love of all things, simultaneously. This recognition is of incoming thoughts instead of those outgoing. There is no intention for analyzing incoming thoughts until they have been registered for processing. Outgoing thoughts are processed in response to those that have already come in.

This means that incoming thoughts are *attentional*, and outgoing thoughts that have been processed are *intentional*. So, the more I concentrate on my *intention* to process thoughts for going out, the more I am not paying *attention* to the incoming thoughts; and as a result, downsizing my awareness of the incoming flow of U-Love.

As I cut off the stream of incoming thoughts, I am also cutting off receiving all the behaviors of the Father that are needed to support my overall well-being and thus cutting off my physical senses as well. If I reverse this, I will be more aware of the incoming U-love than my intent to process outgoing thoughts.

Unseen Forces

The flow of this Universal Love is delivered to the senses via signals from unseen forces of microscopic character such as *photons* for sight and *sound waves* for hearing. Activity within each of these forces creates a polarity that is interpreted as *love* shared between male and female characters. Objects and live-beings of reality use photons and sound waves from two directions: incoming and outgoing. We are aware of sight and hearing via the incoming signals, but not the outgoing. And since the incoming signals carry U-Love, we will get love even when we are not aware of it.

In the past, these forces may have been considered forms of a mystical or religious phenomenon, connecting us to our origin. Here in modern times, however, we understand these to be physical and biological facts of how life here on earth truly works.

Is it Love?

Enlightenment of the Father's presence is subtly delivered by his Universal element of Love. Yet, during very *active* sessions of Love-Now meditation, a very strange phenomenon takes place, twisting your conscious into believing that objects of reality may not always seem as real as the love that is delivering them. This may be better understood by pulling back awareness of the individual objects and paying more attention to all things in reality loving you, all at once.

For those who are older, there also may be times that you will not recognize this to be love. Children, on the other hand, will most definitely realize this love once they've experienced the presence of the Father.

All said, if you don't like the word *love*, you can always create your own term, such as *joy of life; happiness; or your dead ancestors communicating to you from heaven.* It does not make any difference what label it has, because it will come to you whether you are aware of it as love or not.

Coordinating U-Love

While using the live-meditation method of Universal Love, I was not so intent on processing expectations but instead paid more attention to being entertained by the newness and wonder of a joyful reality. This is when I realized the 'joy of life' dominates the 'process of reason.' And, within the reality of U-Love, I was grounded to an all-so-familiar home base in the *aura of the Divine*.

This Universal Love is the incoming flow of thought from reality that introduces a natural meditation, energizing you with the original sense of life, by awakening the senses with all the behaviors of the Father.

Whether you are solitary or interacting with others, through this live-meditation, you'll learn to coordinate U-Love with all the applications of life, while you are doing them: such as, playing, working, reading, and writing.

Results of Live-Meditation

Imagine having an intimate relationship with your surroundings, where all things create and broadcast an aura of love. Each physical sense, every breath you take and move you make, and yes, every thought you think, is loved by all of reality.

The conscious mind focuses on incoming thoughts of Universal Love, while the body is sensing submission and relaxation as a result of that love. These two harmonizing conditions happen simultaneously as one continuous process. And, you won't have to rationalize the results of live-meditation since the results happen automatically as you become a magnet for love.

Self-righteousness, anger, inhibition, fear, uncontrollable mind-chatter, and egotistical activity will be surrendered and replaced by the joy of life; a superior sense of intelligence and deliberation; a keen awareness for the organization and spatial relationship of objects of reality; and a shameless, resilient sense of confidence. All the foregoing attributes will be clarified and exalted

The Origin comes Alive 185

through this simple live-meditation exercise of Love-Now.

I never found it necessary to bow, kneel, chant, believe in, and pray to an unseen God via ritual-worship, or sit blanking-out reality in a deep meditative-like trance when I used this live-meditation method as an alternative for achieving enlightenment. But because certain ritual methods are somewhat effective, they can still be used as a primer to enhance the mood before "going live." However, the results in some respects might be closely the same if ritual methods are not used. This is because the live-meditation method integrates results with live actions of all life applications, instantly—which is the goal of ritual methods in the first place.

While practicing this for several minutes, every so often; I discovered that *I don't do life...life does me!* I also found that *I wasn't worshiping the origin of my alive experience...I was living it!* It was an intimate relationship and cooperative agreement between me and my reality of all things, polarized in love.

My sister and I both agree that this appears to be the most likely way to establish a continuous practice for growing children who will inherit future civilization. Of course, in the case of children, the ultimate result of live-meditation is to see the presence of the Father as he appears from behind the mask of reality to show off his Universal Love. This is when the Father is realized as "The One" unifying sameness and origin of all things.

We are always connected to our origin whether we realize it or not. It's simply a matter of realizing this special connection through Love-Now meditation.

9
Into the Future

Contemplating the Limits of Extreme

Throughout history, we've evolved from simple human beings into complex thinking machines highly capable of mass communication by means of virtual awareness. Could it be that the next stage of this evolution will take us from a socially aggressive society into one of peaceful harmony, by communicating not so much in virtual reality, but more through direct contact with the origin of life?

We've learned that the Divine Presence, showing off as a fatherlike identity in objects of reality, is only for helping newborns realize their first step into life. Viewing this closer, we find this is more about connecting with the *center of the self* to adjust original consciousness from within. Here is a real, viable reason to recall the presence of the Divine Father-deity many times throughout an entire lifetime rather than during childhood only. The Father's presence is a very grown-up experience, and because adults might need help with social issues more than kids, it almost makes more sense to do this at older ages than younger.

However, it's understandable for kids to walk around in their *daddy world* as a toddler, yet highly unlikely they would carry this occasional presence of the Father up into adulthood. This may best be suited to those in a religious cult living in a monastery up in the mountains rather than trying to blend it into a society confused with conformist issues of "work-a-day" attitudes where it might be considered inappropriately unacceptable.

Rather than for adults to try to see the presence of the Father-deity, it might be more realistic to regularly meditate on this memory as a helper to bring about the *aura of the Divine* sense of reality, which can be realized over a lifetime.

In any event, because I have brought you this far by explaining the phenomenon of the presence of a Father-deity, we'll take this next step into the future to explore further possibilities, even though some may seem improbable.

Religion

What is the probability that humans could maintain a connection with this Father-deity? Would staying in touch be similar to being in a family, only a really big family with everybody? Religious cults have sprung up all over the place, apparently trying to do something similar because they mistrusted society and all its situations that are so difficult for many to withstand. If this sense of the Divine Presence of the Father could ever be realized by bringing it into common awareness, would more people join these cults and perhaps break away from traditional religious organizations?

Many religions, including these cults, hold a gathering of their congregation at least once a week to confirm their faith in their God through prayer and ritual–worship. Some of these organizations are very adamant about making certain that their children get educated about faith in God by praying regularly. If kids had a choice between, *accepting faith in God through religious ritual–worship or, experience the presence of the Father regularly*, I wonder which one they would choose!

Religious Evolution

This religion thing has been the same idea for thousands of years, so maybe it's time to open this up and allow it to evolve into something that seems more like a natural occurrence that each one of us can understand and directly connect with, regardless of whether we believe in a God or not. I get a strange feeling that this is exactly how religion and ritual-worship got started and evolved through different denominations.

Religion is not held in high regard in many homes around the world. Maybe what it needs is to advance to the next stage of organization. For this to take place, we won't have to believe through a proxy-awareness of ritual-worship but will have to know about our true origin and how it rises in social consciousness.

Once we have been thoroughly educated about the presence of the Father and know for sure that this is the God religions around the world are talking about, would we still feel a need to attend church? Will all churches shut down and leave the knowledge and training to each family? Or might religious organizations become stronger and attract even larger congregations as a result of *knowing*, rather than merely supporting a *belief* in God?

Back in the Future

Have you ever wondered what the future might be like, living in heaven-on-earth? But a more important question is—what would it take for human civilization to achieve such a tremendous feat? In certain social situations, this kind of ideology might seem to fall somewhere between the impossible and the absurd!

Over the next several–thousand years, what might the future hold for developing kids in a society that would place their sense of origin before all other social conformist activities? Could kids grow up able to build airplanes, ships, and cities while socializing with the origin of life? Or would they simply reject difficult applications of society and accept a fun, easy life of just sitting around passively enjoying the day like a bunch of monkeys? Could they live totally integrated with the Father's presence or just occasionally touch base with him to naturally repair, update, or rejuvenate their physical and psychological systems?

These and other questions border on the ability of such a society to effectively communicate and agree upon common values. This might begin by accepting the condition of life from its inception; a proposition of the human social origin that realigns all the original behavioral elements of the Father as our guide through life—and then everything will be perfect...

But compared to the confused state of society, the only thing that seems to remain constantly perfect is the Divine Presence of the Father. Through this comparison, we also discover the point where heaven and reality collide, and consequently, learn how imperfect life really is. We are now fraught with the distinct possibility that all of us must learn how to survive in a reality of imperfection.

But would it be possible to turn this around? Unfortunately, since physical survival can conflict with the conscious of origin, this would take a tremendous effort—of course until the time comes when we finally resolve this and begin living in a heaven-on-earth environment!

Limitations

It would seem that we'd suffer from certain limitations while trying to build a society using a direct relationship to our original center-of-self. Would decisions made differ from those in society today? Can we add more and more applications without them completely overshadowing our awareness of the Father as the patriarch and origin of all life? And what is the likelihood that civilization could accomplish such a transformation? Would life be repressed by social attitudes and stifle any future development of civilization with this sense of origin? This Divine Presence of reality is seen as a very alive, happy, and positive experience, yet, at the same time, naturally peaceful and often slow. Could human beings revert to this after living in an aggressive society for thousands of years?

There may be no good answer! Nevertheless, here are a couple of examples that might be of interest concerning the ability of a person who occasionally bonded with the Father.

Examples

My brother Locean began to learn simple things about life right after birth and advanced his understanding of these things as he grew: He learned what objects of his new reality were there for and how to use them, but also progressed to develop an awareness of acquiring knowledge through attending school and becoming involved in other interesting activities with friends.

Being involved in social conformist activities did not inhibit his ability to regularly bond with the Father. It only did while he was concentrating on each activity. As long as there was time to relax and submit the thoughts of a day's activities, he was still capable of being drawn into the Father's presence.

You may have heard stories of child virtuoso violinists, pianists, and others who seem to possess uncanny talents for accomplishing things that might take some of us literally a lifetime to achieve. If you think about it, just learning a language from not knowing anything at all, seems an incredible feat within itself. This may be attributed to their ability to frequently, and subconsciously, connect with their origin.

If all things in life truly were created from the Father's behavioral principles (as has been pointed out), then we should be even more competent in our abilities to build a future than if we never practiced recognition of these principles regularly. This is exactly what religions try to do when they attract people to come to church at least once a week to reaffirm their association with the basic principles of their origin. In this same way, what is proposed here is not much different from what religions established long ago.

This foregoing scenario shows that a person—at a time in life who still had a close awareness of his sense of origin—could very easily contribute to building a civilization from thoughts acquired through the meditation of the Father, as well as those learned from society. If children can do this during their younger years, would they be able to continue this up through adulthood? If they could, it would seem that their acquired skills and knowledge of social activities would be at least as strong, or maybe even stronger, than in a society without this awareness at all.

The Transformation

The transformation of a society from what it is now into a 'Divine Presence conscious society' might be very difficult. We would have to learn to coordinate conformist, social activities with the manner of our origin. But it won't happen at all if someone doesn't expose the possibilities of a transformation, in the first place. This presents a tremendous challenge because this has never been done before.

To most of you, this may seem like some kind of fantastic impossible dream, like a fantasy. It's hard to imagine, after all, we've been through since the beginning of time that we could ever transform civilization into a situation where everyone is living in heaven, right here on earth. But it might happen, starting one person at a time, in much the same way religion began—we'd just pick up where religion has left us.

If this transformation were to take place, it would more than likely take thousands of years to mature and manifest, progressively, one person at a time, until most children in their early years have developed enough understanding to retain the memory of their childhood experiences of the Father's presence...and then the next generation would retain this memory up to age twelve...the next to age thirty...and so on. Children would grow more closely matched with a 'sense of belonging' to a Divine-Father throughout a lifetime in society.

This seems to be a very realistic and practical approach, allowing future generations to gradually alter the attitudes of social systems by evolving through the knowledge of their true social origin. But, as much as is known about all this, if this evolution ever comes to pass, it will undoubtedly not take place solely by what they know, but moreover, through the manner in which it is accomplished.

Hidden in Plain Sight

The *presence of a Father-deity* is seen in objects of reality, on occasion, by children from birth up to five years of age and even for years thereafter. This presence is perfectly silent, has no physical form, is neither dark nor light, and is very passive and elusive to the active state of mind of the social conformist. To those who can't see it, it is hidden in plain sight, right before your very eyes..."If it were a snake, it would bite you!"

After this presence disappears, an *aura of the Divine* (a residual sense of this Father-deity presence) can be prominently retained throughout life by children and adults alike. This sensation owns a vitalizing sense of inner-peace, actively broadcast out to one's immediate surroundings, brightening the aura of reality.

The above observations should signal to us all that something else is going on beyond what is commonly known about a God of origin. If you have any reservations about the ability of civilization to move into the next stage of the human endeavor, by meditating a conscious for his Divine Presence, you might want to look around and see how others might be living in the above-described situations. It should be noted that this subject has no business being ignored by a civilization populated with millions of people living their lives from this presence of origin right in front of us, every single day!

Don't Have to Do It!

Taking all this too literally and sitting around *trying* to see the Father in objects of reality will not produce anything, except maybe drive you crazy! Trying is like a *want*; like something expected. *Expectancy* is not a practical application that will bring forth this presence. And so, for adults, once the memory of one's origin has been forgotten, there may be no turning back. This is somewhat comforting because one could only imagine how difficult it would be to return to a life directly connected to the Divine Presence after being put through the trials of society for many years.

Although Melina and I had the same experiences as famous prophets of the past, we never considered ourselves to be Messiahs—forming a new religion or cult from our understanding of the presence of the Father—but merely saw it as a natural biological function that occasionally arose within the conscious to reaffirm the original love and order of life. Keeping this in mind, and now as grown adults, we are challenged with the thought that it's not self-serving salvation that is important, but the growing experiences of children that will reshape the future of civilization. Through these notes, our memory and knowledge about the Divine Presence of the Father are passed on to them.

10
Purpose

You may not truly know that there is a God; however, you should know about the presence of the Father known so well by children in their younger years. This book offers just a glimpse into the beginning; a rebirth in the discovery of the human social origin and might be the closest you'll ever come to realize the truth of life.

By understanding the sense of the reality of the Father, you'll be able to grasp all this much better than if you were left with only having to believe and take a guess at what it's all about.

These are the accounts of a Divine Presence of a fatherlike Deity that Melina and I experienced, on occasion, throughout our younger years. If more understanding should ever be discovered of all this, any future knowledge will be defined by those who would have these same experiences in daily life. Nonetheless, for now, this book can only take the first step by presenting the awareness of a Father-deity through our memories and cannot assume any knowledge of it acquired through studies in theology, religion, physics, or psychology. At this point, the best we can do is, very simply, tell you what it looks like.

For adults, you will only know of the presence of the Father either, by remembering or if someone jogs your memory. If you can't remember, this book is here for you and your children. But it's only the beginning of a journey that will ultimately lead to more understanding. It's sort of like building a house; we're showing you how to drive the first nail, and then it's up to you to show others.

This book presents three questions:

1. Does a fatherlike Deity really exist in our surrounding reality?

2. Could adults create a *heaven on earth* by connecting with the Father as children do in their early years?

3. Would this idea of maintaining a connection to a Divine origin serve any practical purpose for human civilization?

The Origin comes Alive 203

Objectives:

1. To provide a text for parents so they have a good understanding of this subject to discuss with their kids.

2. To develop a common awareness among children so they will remember and retain a sense of belonging to the Divine Presence of the Father throughout their entire lives.

3. To suggest that the *joy of life* be dominant over the *process of reason.*

4. To learn differences and similarities between the presence of the Father and religious terminology; for *Believers in God* to learn what they are worshiping; and for Atheists to learn what Believers are worshiping.

5. The next time you hear a child say *dada*, remember this book... Better yet, remember your own experiences in the presence of the Father.

Surprise!

At the very moment, this memory was recovered; the thought of *the presence of the Father* came as a complete surprise! One could only imagine that for some of you, all of this has come as a pleasant surprise as well. But for others, it may seem quite a progressive departure from conventional wisdom—not to mention a rather radical awakening. In any case, even if these notes hadn't been released when they were, it would have been only a matter of time before this was uncovered and introduced to the public.

At age–one, children with this memory could have told you most of this if only they had understood a colloquial language and how to effectively communicate. But most of all, they would have if given the educational reasoning to make it even worth talking about.

Epilogue for Eternity

Way back before life itself, as a Deity and lonely thought in a dark place, what I wanted more than anything was, entertainment! It should be evident to all that this one, single idea is what brought forth the creation of an arena where life could be realized by a multitude of creatures sharing this new life in joyous celebration.

But life here on earth, as it has turned out, is not always a joyful playing field. It's often like playing a game that, at times, can even get rude when a beautiful life goes bad—like animals preying on each other for their survival. Even though the preyer and preyee ultimately find themselves at opposite extremes of the joy of life, ironically, they share one common value: both are entertained by the fact that life is for enjoying and would do just about anything to maintain this ideal—even kill for it!

Although humans have been endowed with intelligence greater than that of their animal ancestors, they have instinctively taken after them in somewhat the same way. To survive, they protect their land and social customs by maiming and killing each other over simple values of life. Through this basic instinct to survive, the original behaviors of life have been disturbed, confusing thoughts of love and compassion for one another and all things here on earth. After enjoying the pure-love of the Father in one's early years, it is inconceivable how atrocities such as these could ever have taken place—but they have!

Correcting these horrible acts of life might not be possible for the lesser members of the animal kingdom, but for humans, this should be the foremost quest for future generations. They know it is possible through loving relationships that all people can learn to adapt and get along with each other in the face of almost any kind of adversity. It is apparent they are still learning how to behave as humans in their new role as domain keepers of planet earth.

In an attempt to prove that they can rise above their basic animal instincts, they've succeeded in building all manner of things like cities that tower toward the sky; ships and airplanes for travel and commerce; created computers and a virtual computer internet that is rivaled only by their own ability to think and communicate; and flown to the moon and back on a quest to explore and eventually populate the universe outside of their earth. These things thought impossible a thousand years ago are now commonplace in an environment where they can create and build just about anything they can think up.

While chasing the dream of building a better place to live and play, earth's dominant animal specie has worked tirelessly to accomplish total agreement and loving harmony amongst one another, the world over. To undertake this "feat of magic" they have lauded themselves as saints, kings, and scholars to set standards of behavior, by organizing religious beliefs and arguing politics until it seems there is no end in sight, yet have failed in reaching a goal of peaceful coexistence that will propel civilization into the next stage of the human endeavor.

Throughout all the things they have worked toward and accomplished within the timeline of human history, it is obvious that no parent sat down and had a good intelligent talk with their child about the presence of the Father... And though, as unbelievable as this may seem, it is apparently true!

Until they can connect this "missing link" and restore to their conscious, a sense of the Divine Presence known so well in their early years, they will more than likely carry on, as usual, orphaned from their source of life, and thoughts of this beautiful experience may become lost forever in the challenges of time to remain entombed in the silence of memory, literally, as the vanishing point of life, keeping them entertained for eternity playing a never-ending game of hide-and-seek with the conscious of their origin.

It's been a long time coming since the dawn of human beings. They've learned a lot over time on their quest to discover the meaning of life. Scientific and religious perspectives have exhausted the exploration of the origin of humankind, only to stop at the doorstep in getting them to realize where they all come from. They will only see the truth in this when they open the door, look inside, and remember.

The time has now come to place this memory on the path to the future and awaken their social conscious with the spirit of life, by breaking the silence of their origin. Then, they can begin to share this very special memory locked deep inside each and every one, and at last, come away with a more complete understanding and meaningful purpose of the total human experience.

The Origin Comes Alive

At Home with the Divine Presence

Glossary

Definitions according to this Book

aura: an atmosphere or character sensibility about reality.

aura of the divine: an atmosphere of an unseen character or 'Divine Presence' of origin (the Father) who is in charge of communicating an aura of love about one's immediate surroundings; a family-like love of reality.

chromosome: an element in the nucleus of body cells that holds DNA; a processor enabling heredity information in DNA to be communicated throughout the body; sex chromosomes determine sex as either male or female; see *DNA*.

deity: thing of origin; the divine; a supreme-being that is all-knowing and seeing; a single character identification of multiple behaviors; creator; controller of thought; official moderating the thoughts of its creations; see *father*.

dada: baby talk derived from the original sound "aa" that evolved into "da" said as two separate sounds repeated, e.g., da-da; the first identifiable word of life; divine presence; see *father* and *deity*.

father: genetic male, masculine identity; creator; initiator; life-generating force; beginning of human life; original human identity; human operating system; thought controller; a child's first thought; male parent; pa, papa, dada, daddy, and maybe even goo-goo and aa-aa; see *deity*.

fatherlike identity: a multiple behavior identity of masculine authoritarian and analytic characteristics dominating yet complementing its minor feminine behavior; see *father* and *deity*.

God: see *father* and *deity*.

genetic: reproductive, inherited traits determined from family ancestry or origin; hereditary information held in DNA; See *DNA*.

heaven: a tranquil state of mind; vision of a white cloudy blanketed womb-like surround of feminine love with a dominant fatherlike identity as the center of focus; ecstasy with the Father; white cocoon.

identity: identification, awareness, recognition.

imprinting: copying an experience in reality to one's memory.

meditation: an exercise clearing thoughts from the mind; feelings of calm surrender that result in quieting the mind and creating a relaxed sense of stillness about reality.

mirroring: thoughts brought forth from the memory that appear to be reflected by objects of reality; the deity seeing himself as a father-identity in objects of reality.

motherlike identity: multiple behaviors of feminine love and communication characteristics dominating yet complementing its minor masculine behaviors.

ritual: pattern of ceremonial acts; religious rules actively repeated.

polarity: activity created between two opposing forces.

reality: physical surroundings; the existence of life.

DNA: deoxyribonucleic acid; heredity material in body cells.

ESP: ExtraSensory Perception; telepathy; sensing communication thoughts that can't be seen.

FOS: Father Operating System; original thought controller for the operation of life; see *"GM"*.

GM: Genetic Memory; heredity traits; principal thoughts one is born with; see *DNA*.

PTP: Progressive Thought Processing; an active progression of thought.

SCS: Shame through Conformity Syndrome; personal shame carried throughout life.

Research Sources

THE HUMAN GENOME PROJECT: www.genome.gov
A very involved study in genetic research.

INTRODUCTION TO ASTRONOMY:
by Iain Nicholson, Academic Press Ltd 2014.
A rather detailed yet broad view of the nature of the universe.

A GUIDE TO THE ZOHAR - by Arthur Green,
2004 Stanford University Press
Insights into Jewish Kabbalah of The ZOHAR by Matt.

THE COMPLETE WORKS OF LAO TZU - Tao Teh Ching and Hua Hu Ching: by Hua-Ching Ni, SevenStar Communications 1979-2000. Ancient Chinese philosophy of the Universal Way.

THE HOLY BIBLE: King James Version (NKJV) or (AKJV) www.biblegateway.com
History and teachings of Christianity.

BIBLICAL ARCHAEOLOGY SOCIETY:
www.biblicalarchaeology.org –
www.deadseascrolls.org.il
Judaism and Christian archeological findings; includes translations from *The Dead Sea Scrolls.*

THE UNIVERSE IN A SINGLE ATOM:
by The Dali Lama – 2005-2006, Crown Publishing Group, The Convergence of Science and Spirituality.

Contents Detail

THE ORIGIN COMES ALIVE	III
CONTENTS	VI
INTRODUCTION	VII
1 A SENSE OF CREATION	1
2 REMEMBERING THE EXPERIENCE	7
REMEMBERING: A SENSE OF ORIGIN	7
GENDER	9
A SENSE OF MANNER	10
THE LOVE OF LIFE	11
SENSING	11
OUTSIDE SENSE	12
A SENSUAL ORDER	13
RITE OF PASSAGE	14
EXPLANATIONS	15
SUMMARY	18
3 TECHNICAL SENSE	21
BASE MEMORY	21
IMPRINTING TO MEMORY	21
MIRRORING	22
THE SILENT DEITY	23
PROGRESSIVE THOUGHT PROCESSING	24
ESP	25
A TRUE EXAMPLE OF ESP	26

HEALING	27
SUBMISSION	28
THE VANISHING POINT	29
AFTER OUR DESIGN	31
FATHER OPERATING SYSTEM (FOS)	33
HOW DOES IT WORK?	34
FATHERLIKE IDENTITY	35
POLARITY	40
SHORT-CIRCUIT BEHAVIOR	41
GM: GENETIC MEMORY	42
CREATING IDENTITY	46
GENDER IDENTITY	47
THE PROJECTION OF LIFE	49
COMMON PROCESS	51
THE TERRIFIC TWOS	54
MALE AND FEMALE DIFFERENCE	55
IN YOUR DREAMS	56
CONSCIOUS CONFLICT	59
MATCH-MAKING	61
MATCHING FREQUENCY	62
THE CLAY	63
I AM WHO I AM	64
THE SPARK OF CONCEPTION	66
INTERPRETING EXISTENCE	66
ALIVE IDENTITY	68
WHAT'S THE ANSWER?	68
4 LOSING IT	**71**

Trained	72
The Memory Barrier	73
Perception of Reality	74
The Stumbling Block	75
Contest of Conformity	75
A Sense of Shame	77
Shame through Conformity	77
Inside-Out	79
Response Thoughts	80
Senseless	81
Losing by Default	81
No Mirror	82
Baby ID	83
De-Fathering via Mothering	85
Fear of the Unknown	87
The Steps of Knowledge	89
Rules of Nature	90
Orphaned from Our Origin	91
5 RELIGION AND THE ORIGIN	**93**
Charade or Real	94
The Difference	95
Make-Believe	98
Ancient Ritual Fear	99
The Mood of Ritual	101
Belief, Faith, and Hope	102
Prayer	104

THE CHURCH	106
THE HOLY GHOST	107
CHILDREN OF GOD	108
GOD LOVES YOU	109
GOD IS WATCHING YOU	111
FALL FROM GRACE	111
LENT	112
THE RAPTURE: COCOONED	114
GIVING-UP LIFE	115
WOMAN MADE FROM MAN	117
GOD THE DELIVERER	118
IMAGE OF THE FATHER	119
GIVING THANKS	119
THE SOUL	121
ETERNAL LIFE	121
RELIGIOUS SIMILARITIES	123
KEEPING IT ALIVE	124
THE MISSING LINK	125
6 TALKING TO KIDS	**127**
A RIGHT TO KNOW	128
PROOF THROUGH MEMORY	129
THE FIRST WORD	130
MYTH OR MEMORY	131
SEEN NOT HEARD	132
CAN'T TALK BACK	133
GENERATION GAP	134

NOBODY'S TALKING	135
POWER TO COMMUNICATE	136
SHAME AND CONFORMITY	136
FEAR OF THE DEITY	137
FAMILY VALUES	138
DRUGS AND KIDS	139
A BIRTHRIGHT	140
ADULT, NOT BABY	141
VIDEOS AND GAMES	141
PARENTS' PRIMARY OBLIGATION	143
7 RATIONALIZING IT	**145**
BONDING WITH THE FATHER	145
CONCEPTION AND MESSIAH	147
THE BURNING HEART	148
REVISITING THE WHITE COCOON	150
OUTSIDE THE BUBBLE	151
REALIZING GOD	153
GOING BACK SALVATION	155
THE GLITCH	157
FAMILIAR CONFORMITY	158
GENETICS	159
TRUST/MISTRUST	160
THE NATURAL INTERNET: PRAYER THEORY	160
HIDE-AND-SEEK	163
SUBMISSION AND PRAYER	163
A SENSE OF TIMELINE	166

LOVE-NOW	168
THE FIRST STEP	171
THE BRIDGE	172
8 LIVE-MEDITATION	**173**
OUTSIDE SOURCES	174
FIRST ACTS OF LIFE	174
UNIVERSAL LOVE	175
PROCESS OF AWARENESS	177
REDIRECTING U-LOVE	178
COMPASSION AND PASSION	178
PREEMPTING LOVE OF LIFE	179
ATTENTION VS. INTENTION	180
UNSEEN FORCES	181
IS IT LOVE?	182
COORDINATING U-LOVE	183
RESULTS OF LIVE-MEDITATION	184
9 INTO THE FUTURE	**187**
RELIGION	189
RELIGIOUS EVOLUTION	190
BACK IN THE FUTURE	191
LIMITATIONS	192
EXAMPLES	193
THE TRANSFORMATION	195
HIDDEN IN PLAIN SIGHT	197
DON'T HAVE TO DO IT!	198

10 PURPOSE	**201**
THIS BOOK PRESENTS THREE QUESTIONS:	202
OBJECTIVES:	203
SURPRISE!	204
EPILOGUE FOR ETERNITY	204
GLOSSARY	**210**
RESEARCH SOURCES	**213**
CONTENTS DETAIL	**214**

www.ingramcontent.com/pod-product-compliance
Lightning Source LLC
Chambersburg PA
CBHW070545010526
44118CB00012B/1229